Walking With The Old Ones: Awakening to Native American Spirituality and Healing

by

Wachetecuma
She Who Heals the Healers

Strategic Book Publishing and Rights Co.

Strategic Book Publishing and Rights Co.
12620 FM 1960, Suite A4-507
Houston, TX 77065
www.sbpra.com

For information about special discounts for bulk purchases, please contact Strategic Book Publishing and Rights Co. Special Sales, at bookorder@sbpra.net.

ISBN: 978-1-63135-491-5   1-63135-491-4

Prologue

In each day comes a magic time, when in the stillness of the morning, washed clean by the glorious light of a distant rising star, time stands still. The small ones, the four-leggeds, and the winged ones speak quietly of many things. They speak of the constancy and beauty of the Mother, and the enduring embrace of the Father, the legacy given by Creator to all—the sacred circle of unending time, and the sure knowledge that all time is all time.

—Wachetecuma

To Native American People:
Hear the call of your Indian blood.
Respond with courage and commitment.
Gratefully welcome Wakan Tanka Tunka Silla.
Trust your Spirit Guides.
Respect the wisdom of the Elders.
Embrace remembered sacred knowledge.
Set your feet soundly upon the Good Red Road.
Walk always in a good way.
-The Old Ones-

<u>To All My Relations:</u>
Hear the call of your blood.
Respond with courage and commitment.
Gratefully welcome Creator.
Trust your Helpers.
Respect the wisdom of the Elders.
Embrace remembered sacred knowledge.
Set your feet soundly upon a good path.
Walk always in a good way.
-The Old Ones-

Acknowledgements

Since the great common denominator in life is love, this book serves to say thank you to all those who have freely loved me and have encouraged this writing in the hope that others may be similarly motivated to trust the path of their individual directions to spiritual awakening.

To the Old Ones, Grandmother Aquilla, the Sha Sha Wan Nee, Stays By Me, Walks Ahead, Walks With Crows, Redwing Blackbird, Young Wolf, Water Beaver Woman, Turtle Woman, Red Shield, and White Elk—thank you.

To the Black Fox Drum, whose dedication and perseverance served to uplift and inspire me at all times—many thanks.

To all the Light Warriors of the world—those who show the way by walking their talk—thank you.

I am known to be a world-class procrastinator. Because of this proclivity, special thanks are due to my sister, brother, and friends because of their unswerving support, which I laughingly dubbed 'creative nagging.' It goes something like this: The phone rings. "Hello."

"Are you writing?"

A prolonged pause follows. "I will be. Writing, that is. Thanks."
—Wachetecuma

Thank You to 'Team Wachetecuma'

My heartfelt appreciation is extended to everyone from Writers Literary Agency & Services, Inc., with special thanks to my Agent, Georgina. The patience, guidance, and friendly professionalism afforded by each of you will not be forgotten.

Thank you so much, Ellen Green, Press Manager from Strategic Publishing, for always going the extra mile.

The on-going dedication evidenced by everyone representing Eloquent Books manifested in a continuous flow of information and interaction, resulting in the successful publication of *Walking With the Old Ones.* Many thanks.

Kira, Art Manager for AEG, Strategic, and Eloquent Publishers deserves a special pat on the back for putting me in touch with Jamie Runyan, from AEG Publishers, whose intuitive expertise helped to bring to light a long-held dream for the cover design.

Special thanks to Cindi Pietrzyk, Edit Manager for AEG Publishing, who has proved to be not only patient, but an especially responsive, caring overseer. Megan Collins, copy editor, reviewed the manuscript with an adept eagle eye to detail, which proved to be a great boon. "SP", Print Manager, AEG Publishing, proved to be the quintessential designer for the formatting of *Walking With the Old Ones.*

I greatly appreciate the endorsement from Rebecca Gearhart, Ph.D., Associate Professor of Anthropology, Chair, Department of Sociology & Anthropology, Illinois Wesleyan University. Dr. Gearhart's endorsement is especially meaningful to me. I have long respected her work and integrity of purpose.

If I have neglected to express appreciation to anyone, please accept my apology. Your input was no less appreciated because of my oversight.

Well done, everyone! Thank you.

—Wachetecuma

Words from Wachetecuma

I have come to The Good Red Road, my personal Native American path to spirituality and healing, through the love and teaching of the Old Ones, with the help of extraordinary teachers and helpers. The Old Ones have encouraged me always, and in all ways, to become who I am today, a sixty-seven year old, mixed-blood Native American woman. I make no claim to being more or less than I am. I am not a numbered or registered member of any tribe or group. I represent only myself, through my life experience, and by passing along information the Old Ones wish to share.

With a few notable exceptions, I have sought to protect the privacy of those mentioned in *Walking With the Old Ones* by changing names, using Indian names not widely known, or by using a designate such as Shaman, rather than a name.

I have striven to bring forth the true events told in this non-fiction narrative, exactly as they happened, with the exception of implementing small changes to enhance understanding. Occasionally, I changed or left out a small part of a ceremony. This was done at the behest of the Old Ones, solely to protect the integrity of the ceremony.

In the spirit of the Grandfathers and Grandmothers, those who have gone before, those who are still working for the betterment of all people, it is the great honor of This One not only to serve as a Hollow Bones for healings performed by the Old Ones, but to share their words of encouragement and wisdom with you, the reader.

May you walk always in beauty.

—Wachetecuma

Table of Contents

15

The Teachings of the Shoshone Woman

My grandmother was dead. Of course, I knew that my grandmother was dead. And yet, here she was, seated facing me, legs tucked comfortably beneath her in the tall, soft grass—and she was smiling.

I smiled back. It was an automatic response. I had been smiling at my Grandmother since my birth—and I loved the warm, liquid mystery of her dark eyes, smiling back at me. There was a whole world of depth and knowledge shining in those eyes, knowledge beyond my meager child's ability to understand.

As Grandmother and I sat quietly, adjusting to the newness of our situation, I thought about the time of her crossing, and tried to find a way to understand. My grandmother was dead—but was not!

As a child, This One was always aware that she was not like others. There were things she remembered—her own birth, flashes of light from before her birth, intrinsic understanding and love of Mother Earth and Father Sky. Her world was peopled by four-leggeds and winged ones living in the natural harmony of prey and predator. All of these things she was aware of, and more. She loved this place, this physical place, this natural place in time, and was aware all the while, as her grandmother had taught her, that all time is all time. She was isolated by circumstance and geography, isolated by her parents' alcoholism and the inevitable resultant poverty and degradation. There was also degradation of spirit, though this was rarely felt by the child. Rather, the child went her own way, happy in the ways of her own self, her personal, private world, her own learning.

The child's grandmother was called Aquilla. To the child, she became known as The Shoshone Woman, and, by example, she became her teacher and mentor. From her grandmother, the child learned to be proud without ego, to be straightforward, honest, to practice patience and endurance, to know love. She has no memory of the grandmother ever complaining, even when she lay dying in terrible pain. No one in the family ever told the child that native blood coursed through her veins, along with blood from other lines; but, she always knew and, in childhood games of cowboys and Indians, she always insisted on 'being the Indian.'

Then one terrible day, the child's grandmother crossed, and was gone from this physical place. Though she had, with cold tears coursing down her face, dug little graves out of the freezing ground for deceased barn cats, truly the child had no real understanding of death. She only knew she had lost her best friend, the person in the world who loved her wholeheartedly and without reservation. The Shoshone Woman died in November. A dreary and subdued winter followed.

But, at last, spring returned. Trees leafed out, grass grew lush and green once more, and spring flowers peeped their heads up to see if it was yet time to bloom. Sun warmed the child's face as the sound of the little winged ones went about their work. Life was once more good; all of sleeping, dormant, nature was now awake —resurrected. It was then that The Shoshone Woman came to be with This One.

Throughout the gauzy, surreal summer that followed, we sat under the big tree in the front yard, the Shoshone Woman and I. We talked of many things, of the old ways, and the people, and all that had been lost. Sometimes we were sad that all was not as it had once been; sometimes, we laughed and reminisced about good times, losing ourselves in the past. We sat on a blanket of Kentucky blue grass, as she taught me. Our lives seemed to be spun out in slow motion, like the nearly invisible spider webs that trail out for long distances on the autumn winds, like silken threads connecting all things. So it was with us, as I continued to live and learn in this timeless summer cocoon of spirituality.

And then one day, it was autumn, and she was gone. Not really gone, of course, but gone in the wonderful way I had come to know her over the summer. Never again would I know her in quite the same way, but she is with me still, in spirit always, and in all ways. She had taught me what was needed and, like any good parent or grandparent, stepped aside to allow the young one to go forth alone, having gained the knowledge and strength to stand independently.

I have no conscious memory of all that was taught to me that summer, but the knowledge within me directed, shaped, defined, redefined, and refined me over the course of years until it was once more time for me to come back to my true path, my Good Red Road.

Not surprisingly, this came about in an odd way.

The Onset of Disease

I was married. My husband and I had it all. We were the leaders of the pack—in our own circle—and we were so immersed in each other, in love with love; as I said, we had it all. We were complete unto ourselves, a whole and invincible male female polarity of power. My husband was the president of a spin-off unit to a powerful parent company, headquartered in a distant city. My husband was the company wunderkind, the fair-haired golden boy; he was young, good-looking, over-the-top bright, and very well educated. He excelled in every phase of operation concerning the company—management, labor, finance, public relations—and he was particularly good at hands-on management. No problem was too great, too challenging, or too obscure. If my husband were unable to immediately solve a problem, he would improvise until he found the proper answer. I was very involved and aware of my contribution to his success. I was the perfect corporate wife, hosting intimate get-togethers, as well as large parties, with equal finesse. I made it my business to know of any problems, or potential problems, involving company operation and particularly personnel. I charmed corporate executives and local employees alike so that my husband's ship could sail on in calm waters, known waters. I always kept my 'ear to the ground' on his behalf, on our behalf. And for a long time, life was good—or so it seemed. I was my husband's recognized, respected partner. But somewhere along the line, I lost his love. I always thought perhaps he had come to believe his own press, and it went against him—and us. I became ill.

This illness came about in small ways in the beginning and took place over the course of several months. A series of three small events precluded my illness. I was involved in a martial arts class. After 'missing' a fall, in spite of a thick, padded protective mat, I hit my head on the floor with such force that I lost my hearing for five hours—entirely. I may have suffered a concussion, as well, but I have never been big on doctors, hospitals, and traditional medicine in general. So I saw no medical personnel, and no X-rays were taken. And my hearing returned. The next event was also a small accident. Competing in a nighttime tennis tournament for mixed doubles, I took a strong stance at the net. To end the point, my opponent responded quickly, accidentally spiking a ball directly down onto the little finger of my left hand, breaking it. A friend who acted as umpire stopped play, looked at the finger, and said, "Are you sure it's broken?" I replied in the affirmative, whereupon he said, "Can you move it?" And I could move it, with great pain. He pronounced that the finger was bruised, not broken. My partner and I resumed play, winning our match. The finger quickly turned black and blue and swelled so badly I thought the skin might split open. The following morning, I went to an orthopedic surgeon and he set and splinted the finger. He took an x-ray that showed that the force and angle of the ball hit the finger so hard that a triangle of bone was broken off at the first joint. He said the finger could be straightened, and pinned. I declined. That was the second happening. The third event was more subtle, more obscure, and harder to explain. It came about for two reasons: my disenfranchisement with existing medical practitioners, treatments, and medical facilities; and my ongoing 'I can overcome anything, everything will be fine' optimistic attitude.

Mae Introduces Me To "White Medicine"

Over the course of the next three months, following these first two accidents, I became very lethargic. I had difficulty focusing and could barely stay awake. I was also very weak. The least little thing became a tremendous effort. At the onset of this steadily declining physical state, I was able to pace myself and do small things at the house—laundry, cooking, cleaning,—regular household maintenance. I was still able to drive the car out to do grocery shopping and I visited with friends for short spaces of time.

I slowly 'went downhill,' spending more and more of each day sleeping. I lay cocooned warmly in a blanket on the couch in the living room. When awake, I often watched with lazy, immobile interest the ever-changing shadow designs produced as the sun progressed across the great arch of the sky during the day. It was an altogether surreal experience. I was often conscious of a warm, fuzzy, tingling sensation in my tummy and abdomen. I had no idea at the time that the sensation I was experiencing was caused by internal bleeding. It was not at all unpleasant. Invariably, I drifted into a sort of dream state, where I was aware of sounds going on around me, but they had no meaning for me—they were as background noise, or traffic noise; you hear it, but pay it no attention. So it came to be that I spent much of my time dreaming and seeing visions that were so real, so intense, that these dreams and visions became my reality. I felt very peaceful in this new reality, these visions, very serene and secure in my new world.

I had no appetite. Food was an annoyance to me. At the onset of my illness, I was still able to fix food for my husband, but even then, I barely nibbled it. As time passed, I could not abide the smell of food. Just a whiff of cooking food would cause me to be violently ill. I was not able to keep any food 'down.' At the urging of friends, I tried to eat, and experienced terrible, lacerating pain. The pain was so intense I could barely breathe; it felt like being slashed deep into the stomach and abdomen with dozens of razor sharp knives. In addition to regurgitating everything I ate, and combined with the pain, I began to experience the worst diarrhea imaginable. I was losing weight at the gallop.

As I became more ill, some of my friends tried to help. My friend Mae arrived one morning unannounced, helped me dress, and, ignoring my feeble protests, carted me off to be examined by her personal physician, an old-time country doctor, still practicing in his seventies. Mae was of the same generation, and he had been her physician for thirty years. She totally believed in his ability.

Mae was a sister-friend-mother, all rolled into one. When I first met her, I was working part time at the local library. She was looking for someone to type a handwritten manuscript for a book she was in the process of writing. Although Mae was a good forty years my senior, working together over the course of the next year, we became fast friends, and remained so until the time of her death many years later. Mae was extremely intelligent, a self-taught erudite lady who generated enormous respect. Her quest for knowledge became her touchstone, her lifelong passion. Mae had little formal education, but her dedication and love of learning was so concentrated that she eventually amassed a library containing thousands of books, many of them rare first editions. These were, in great majority, non-fiction books, encompassing a broad spectrum of subjects, all lovingly categorized and cataloged according to the Dewey Decimal System. Mae had read and/or studied them all—science, mathematics, geography, logistics, whatever came to hand. She especially loved the study of anthropology, geology, paleontology, and related subjects. She spent many happy hours ensconced in the quiet and tranquility of her private library.

None of Mae's impressive body of knowledge was a help to us in understanding the illness that was so afflicting me, however, and in spite of her best intentions, her trusted family physician was of no help. I saw him on two separate occasions. The first visit brought forth a vague diagnosis of "female problems," with no specifics, and no treatment recommended. The second visit proved even less satisfying than the first. The kindly old gentleman asked me to take a seat and asked if I were having marital difficulties. He explained that he could see I was "high-strung" by nature, and recommended a mild tranquilizer. Needless to say, I was very discouraged by what I considered to be his cavalier attitude. And I was so very ill. Mentally dismissing the entire medical community as no place to seek help, I returned to my living room couch to help myself the only way I knew how—by mentally surrounding myself with positive thoughts and healing light. I grew weaker.

Alice Saves My Life

The day came when I was unable to rise from my bed, and I spent twenty-three hours a day sleeping or lying in quiet trance-like thought. I had a window in my bedroom that faced onto the patio toward the front entrance to the home. One day, the mailman had a tire blow out in the driveway to our home. I heard the blowout with only the vaguest comprehension. The mailman, a gentleman I had known for years, rang the bell, asking to use the phone. I called out to him, telling him I was ill, but to come into the house and use the phone on the desk in the living room. These were the days before the advent of the cell phone, and obviously, these were also the days when folks didn't feel the need to lock their doors. He asked if I needed help, and I replied that I was fine, just a little 'under the weather.' I heard him use the phone, then close the outside door as he left the house. He thanked me from the patio, and said he hoped I would soon be better. I wasn't.

I continued to decline. It seemed to me that the weaker my body became, the stronger my mind became, and I continued to maintain my life-long optimism. Everything was very sharp to me now; everything was very clear. All of my senses were heightened, almost euphoric. At times I felt quite removed from my body, as if my spirit were flying free, and at these times I experienced no pain, just a timeless sense of being. And then one day as I lay in bed, covered with three blankets and a bedspread, I began to shake with cold. I shook until my teeth chattered. The temperature outside was nearly eighty degrees Fahrenheit. And I was suffering from extreme hypothermia. I thought about what to do. I knew I was in great danger, that my poor, wasted body had no energy left with which to fight. My mind and great strength of will, I realized, were the only tools available to me to save my life. Mustering all my remaining energy, I tried to double the blankets over me, and, not having enough strength to do this, bunched them closer together to make a thicker mass, as best I could. I then got completely under the blankets, head and all, rolling into a fetal position to generate what body heat I could manage to my vulnerable core area, drawing the blankets as close about me as possible.

With my head under the blankets, in total darkness, time because a floating, gauzy reality. I had no idea how long I stayed curled into this position. I tried to focus, to sustain myself with healing light, and indeed I seemed to be surrounded with pink, white, and golden light. I smiled with joy as I observed in a detached way, as these healing 'friends' danced and swirled like small aurora borealis around the huddled figure under the blankets. But my body was still shuddering with cold. My teeth were still chattering. I decided I needed to think warm thoughts. I thought about the hottest days of summer I could remember. I tried to envision the desert with heat waves shimmering over it. I tried to imagine a sidewalk so hot in the blistering heat of noon that you could 'fry an egg' on it. After a time, I became aware of being just a tad warmer. Perhaps my body heat had increased by being totally under the blankets, or perhaps the combination of my visual imagery and healing energy worked just a little. At any rate, I fell into a light sleep, exhausted from my efforts to sustain myself. As I drifted off, I was aware that I might just keep drifting and not 'come back.' It was almost a neutral feeling; I knew that, physically, I might not be able to live, and I was comfortable with the thought in an abstract way, but somewhere deep within me, I hoped I would be able to continue.

"Hello! Hello. Is anybody home?" I was jarred to consciousness by the sound of a lady's voice calling to me from the patio. I struggled to get my head clear of the blankets, and called out, "I'm here." But my voice was too weak to be heard. Presently, I heard her call out once more, while knocking on the door. "Hello. Is anyone here?" I heard, in my neighbor's voice, the sound of salvation. With all of my strength, I called out, "Please come in. I'm sick." And that is how I met Alice, a neighbor who had recently moved into the area.

Moments later, Alice appeared in the doorway to the bedroom, saying, "I'm sorry to just barge in like this, but I haven't seen you lately, and I was concerned. When we first moved next door, I used to see you coming and going all the time." Resting between breaths, I told Alice about the hypothermia I was experiencing. She asked me what she could do to help me. I asked her to get me into the bathtub and begin running warm water, gradually increasing the heat of the water, as I was able to tolerate it. After a time, I began to feel warmer, stronger. What an unusual first meeting! There is no doubt in my mind that Alice was sent to save my life that day. Once out of the bath, she called her husband and asked him to bring their car over to the house. She then bundled me into a clean nightgown, socks, and a fleecy comforter. Her husband then carried me to their car and they drove me to a hospital clinic to meet a doctor of whom they had heard good things. Ultimately, that amazing doctor proved to be my salvation. But I insisted on returning home from the clinic that day, still positive that I could recover 'on my own.' My parents lived several states away from my husband and me. Finally, in desperation, my husband asked my mother to come for an extended stay with us and attempt to "talk some sense into me." My husband and my mother strongly felt I was in need of hospital care and lost no opportunities for expressing themselves. I was annoyed and felt 'put upon' by their constant pressure. Ignoring their concern, I continued to rely on treatment guidelines from a very good friend, a dietitian who, though she continued to support me in all ways, also counseled me to seek 'professional help.' I steadfastly resisted all efforts toward hospitalization, and my friend, understanding my mind-set, did what she could for me in the way of nutrition. Unfortunately, I not only had absolutely no appetite, but on the rare occasions when I was able to swallow a few mouthfuls of food, severe lacerating pain engulfed me immediately. Most times, however, I was simply unable to keep the food down. My friend actually diagnosed my condition before the man who was to become my "white" doctor and my friend had the opportunity to do so.

One morning, I decided to weigh myself, but I needed help to stand, and it was a moment before I could steady myself on the bathroom scales, with Mom pretty well "propping me up." I had to laugh at myself. I was as weak and unsteady as a newborn foal. It took a long moment before I was able to focus enough to read the scales. My weight had dropped more than forty pounds in the preceding three months. At five feet, six inches, I could no longer tip the scale even to one hundred pounds. "Well, that's it, then," I thought. "It's now or never. I'm going to die anyway. I may as well give the white medicine a try."

"Mother," I said, "Would you please call my Doctor and see if he can get me into the hospital? I think I need to go to the hospital now, as soon as possible."

"You think so? Well, it's about time," Mother kidded. "Don't worry, it's all set," she added. "For the past ten days, your doctor has left standing orders at the Emergency Entrance to the hospital for you to be admitted anytime, day or night. All we have to do is show up there."

Grandfather Kee-oh-ta-kah Performs A Healing

When I was admitted to the hospital, tests were administered. I was first taken to a cancer ward, since my diagnosis was not yet completed. Not only had I lost forty pounds, but 87 percent of my muscle definition, as well. I was almost literally down to skin and bones. I had not been able to eat and keep anything down for some time, had no bowel movements, and had severe, lacerating cramps in my stomach and abdomen. I also suffered from some open 'wounds.' Upon learning this, the duty nurse quickly called orderlies to wheel my entire bed, with me in it, and everything in my room to another area away from the cancer ward. My mother, who had come to be with me during this time, told me later that when I was moved from the Cancer Ward to a semi-private room on another floor, she knew then that I would live. Mother's reasoning? I had been born in room 304; the room I was moved to was 304! Mother felt it was a 'sign' for rebirth, a reassurance from our Creator, beyond doubt or question, that I would indeed enjoy a new life from this day forward.

Test results confirmed conclusively what my doctor had suspected—that I suffered Crohn's Disease, a chronic disease of the digestive tract. The disease presents with a variety of symptoms, and each patient is treated according to how the disease impacts him/her individually. In my case, the disease was spread pretty well throughout my system. I was in an extremely weakened and precarious state of health. The course of treatment ordered by my doctor was meant to heal my open wounds, strengthen my immune system, and gradually re-introduce solid foods into my system, if possible. There was some question as to whether or not my digestive process was still workable, whether or not I could eat solid food, and whether or not my system could process it. Immediate hydration of my system was ordered—glucose, lipids, and nutrients.

That night, I lay in the soft shadowed quiet of my hospital bed, warm, and very, very, still. Medication to my open wounds had eased the hurt, and I drifted in and out of reality, periodically aware of muted conversation. I listened intently, trying hard to focus so that I might hear what the voices were saying, but whoever was speaking was just beyond my hearing range. In my unfocused way, I was mildly irritated by not being included. Of course, no one was there. No one was there in this physical reality, at any rate. My mind wandered in a lazy fashion, a forum for review and consideration. I was aware from talking to my doctors, and even more aware on an intrinsic level, that whether or not I was strong enough to survive could go either way. I felt at ease with either reality. And yet, I felt compelled toward the choice of living. In the dim recesses of my conscious mind, I really wanted to live. Through all the ups and downs of everyday life and living, with the tragedy and joys, the triumphs and defeats, I have always recognized living for the great wellspring of joy that it is. I wake up every morning, elated to be alive. I thought about how I might help myself, and all of a sudden, I knew what to do. It made me sad to think of not living here anymore. So I called for a Medicine Man.

And Grandfather Kee-oh-ta-kah suddenly appeared before me. I was aware that he was a Spirit Grandfather. I felt his love and power envelop me at once. I knew no fear; I felt so wonderfully warm and cared for. He was striking in appearance. The right side of his face, except for a white circle around the eye, was painted entirely black. The left side of his face, except for a black circle around the eye, was painted entirely white. Where the black and white paints met under his jawbone, a black stripe of paint ran straight down the middle of his bare chest, where it disappeared under the top of his buckskin colored breechclout. From his ear down his left arm, a black stripe ran to the end of his middle finger, and from his ear down his right arm, a white stripe ran to the end of his middle finger. Around his neck, Grandfather wore a necklace of bear claws. His bare chest was covered only by an open leather vest ornamented by two segmented deer horn 'buttons.' His long black hair was plaited into two thick braids wrapped tightly with strips of rawhide. Although the hair was braided all the way up to the ears, the braid wrapping began just above the shoulder, tied about two or three inches from his waist, allowing a 'tail' of hair to flow free below the tie. In his right ear, the Grandfather wore a circular bone earring, accentuating the sweep of his firm mouth and jaw, his high cheekbones. He wore a small ornamental headdress made from black bear fur treated to stand up, and porcupine quills to which very small red feathers had been attached. Two eagle feathers were attached with a deer antler button to a simple strip of leather fastened about his left bicep. Both his bare torso and arms were strongly muscled. In his left hand, he casually carried a long, slim raised ridge steel blade, 'pinched in' a third of the way up the blade. This blade, affixed at the 'pinched in' surface to a wooden handle with wet-shrunk rawhide strips, was a wickedly formidable-looking tomahawk. In his right hand, Grandfather Kee-oh-ta-kah gently carried three small flowers, one red, one white, and one yellow. As striking and handsome a figure as he presented, the most amazing thing about Grandfather Kee-oh-ta-kah was the sheer intelligence and intensity with which he looked at This One. I was aware of the strength of his warrior energy, the strength of his healing energy, the feeling of love and kindness emanating from him, the overwhelming feeling that all would be well. And so it was.

The Grandfather began by cleansing the room, and all within, with the burning of sacred white sage. He offered gifts of tobacco, and cedar and sweet grass, as he saluted the Four Directions. The Grandfather that night danced, and sang songs of prayer. He covered This One with a buffalo robe, and he touched This One with eagle feathers. He smoked a sacred pipe. He chanted. He drummed. He used shakers as he spoke prayers. He spoke at length to This One in his own language, telling many tales of the people, tales of living, and tales of healing. The linear part of This One did not understand his language; the spiritual part of This One understood everything. He stayed with This One throughout the night and, towards morning, This One slipped into strange and wonderful dreams.

In the morning, when I awakened, the Grandfather had gone. In the sunlit embrace of my blankets, I could still feel his energy, his healing love, and when the day nurse came into the room, I lay there, cozy and warm, gently smiling. I now knew that I was to live, and that my life had purpose. Things were never the same after that, and it was a very good thing, this new path I found myself traveling. My new life had begun.

The War Years

All my life, up to this time of rebirth, I had been conscious of understanding things beyond. With no frame of reference, and no one to talk with about the unusual circumstances of my life, I often found myself confused, and, on occasion, even questioned my own sanity. In those days, I had no words to label what happened to me on a daily basis. Besides remembering my own birth, I also remembered, as a two-year old, 'flying' up and down the stairwell between the main and second floors of the house where we lived, and all around, indoors and out—and then returning to the baby bed where I was supposed to be napping. Right after I learned to talk, I woke up screaming one night, and when Mother came to comfort me, I repeated over and over again, "Daddy is hurt, Daddy is hurt." This was during World War II, and my Father was in a company of Army engineers, building roads and bridges ahead of the front line troops. Consequently, his unit often encountered the first fighting to take place against the enemy. Mother learned that my father had suffered a shrapnel injury to the hand. It was only later when my mother realized that considering the time difference, Dad's injury would have been inflicted at the exact same time I awoke screaming, "Daddy is hurt! Daddy is hurt."

Because, as children, we were blissfully unaware, the days of the War were happy for my little brother and me, but were long and filled with anxiety for the adults involved.

My mother went to work in a war goods factory, and my Grandmother Aquilla, came to live with us, mostly to help care for us kids, but also to share support. Families tended to pull together in those hard times.

As children, however, it was the best of times. We spilled out of our warm beds each day and hurried to wash up in the second-story bathroom, adjacent to our bedrooms, so that we could then hurry to lean on the wide windowsill in the bathroom and wait in the delightful chill of the fresh air of a new morning to watch the train go by on the tracks just a stone's throw from our house. It was such a big train, an old-fashioned train, big and black, and belching coal smoke. And all too soon it vanished, chugging and snorting, from our sight. Our morning routine then concerned what we were to do if a stranger approached us. We were admonished not to get into a car with anyone unless our mother or grandmother was there, and we were taught to recite our name and address in case we got lost. We were told it was okay to talk to a policeman. Following our daily 'safety' talks, we trooped downstairs to share a community breakfast with our playmates, a girl my age and a boy my brother's age, who lived with their parents in the apartment next door. After breakfast, our time was our own. The four of us played the day away until time for lunch and afternoon naps. In the evening, we were tucked into bed to say prayers, and snuggled down with the muted, comforting voices of the adults drifting up from downstairs.

There was an old radio in the home and each evening, before bedtime, we all gathered around to hear Lowell Thomas give the news. A map of Europe was tacked up on the wall with little flags placed here and there. Some nights, as we listened to the news, my mother would go to the map and add another little flag or two to indicate where she thought my Father's unit was deployed. Later on, my mother was at work during the news time, so my grandmother would place the little flags on the map. Mother's factory was within sight of our house, and Grandmother always lifted us up to the window on the first landing of the stairwell to see where Mother was working (actually only the smokestack could be seen) before she took us up to be tucked into bed. Grandmother led us in the Child's Prayer of "Now I Lay Me Down to Sleep." She then always reassured us that Mother would be home when we woke up in the morning. In this way, we lived through the days of World War II, and one day, the lean, handsome man who was our father did, indeed, return home!

Dad's Homecoming

The man Mother fell in love with, however, the idealistic young husband and father with hopes and dreams for a promising future, failed to return from the War. The man who returned had seen too much, observed up close and first-hand man's insane inhumanity to man. He had lost good friends. He had endured unimaginable personal and emotional hardship. As mentioned, Dad's engineering unit was charged with the building of bridges, roads, and airfields to more easily move equipment and combat troops up to the 'front.' This unit was often the first to fall under the devastating firepower of a fierce enemy bent on stopping the work at any cost. The often pensive, occasionally brooding man who returned from the War, however, bore a striking resemblance to the young father and husband, and everyone was thankful for his return. Our small town quickly became aware of Dad's homecoming, and our home became a whirlwind of visiting friends and relatives laughing and talking together, enjoying one another's company at impromptu celebrations.

Country Living

Gradually, life returned to a semblance of normalcy, and our parents made the decision to move to the peace and quiet of the country. Dad returned to work as a carpenter and cabinetmaker, just as he had done before the War. We lived in a nice little rental house with some outbuildings and trees around it, with a nice yard and a big vegetable garden, surrounded by acres and acres of farmland all around. Our nearest neighbor lived on a farm about half a mile away.

My parents had rented the house from folks who had temporarily relocated in Arizona due to health reasons. Some personal possessions remained, however, and I found myself captivated by one corner of the living room where a tall, beautiful, glass-fronted wood cabinet housed several shelves of variously

47

colored books, all neatly arranged. I was entranced. I couldn't take my eyes off these mysterious objects so precisely embossed with black, silver, and gold lettering.

Most mysterious of all, this cabinet was locked! I wanted more than anything in the world to carefully open the big glass-fronted door and remove these magic items, to touch them, to hold them in my hands, to feel their energy, and wait for them to speak to me. Although I was only four years old at the time, I had been learning to read and the need to read these books was a palpable ache in my small being. But such was not to be. "The books," my mother carefully explained to me, "do not belong to us, and we don't have permission to read them."

Undeterred, I spent some time each day, studiously seated on the floor before the bookcase, asking my patient Mother, "Momma, what's this word" as I placed my finger on the glass over a word in a title. "And what's this word? And this one?" Understandably, before long, Mother advised me it was time to go outside to play.

In those days, air conditioning was almost unheard of, especially in private homes, and our home was no exception. Summers were blazing hot, and in the early mornings, when dew still adorned the grass, Mother 'aired out' the house. Shortly, however, she closed doors and opened windows away from the 'sun side' of the house just a crack, no more than an inch, and pulled all the shades down. These were the days of polio, and each afternoon, my brother and I were required to come indoors out of the hot sun and retire to our bedrooms to read, play quietly or lay down for a nap. We were advised to be quiet for a couple of hours during the hottest part of the day. Some nights, after the sun had gone down, it was so close and hot, even at midnight, with all the doors and windows open, that sleep was fitful. On those occasions, we slept in the living room on little pallets, instead of in our hot bedrooms, and throughout the night, I recall awakening briefly to realize that Mother was moving quietly among us, softly bathing our faces and bare arms with cool water.

Those were the days of squeezing a color 'bead' into a sack of oleo, the days of the first French fries made in the home, the days of vats of home-made beer and big stone crocks with home-made pickles 'put down,' of gum called Juicy Fruit, and electric fans.

On my fifth birthday, my 'boyfriend,' Billy, who lived on the farm half a mile away, gave me the biggest strawberry from his mother's garden, a pack of Juicy Fruit gum, and a kiss on the cheek for my birthday presents. Billy and his brothers and sisters were frequent guests in our home, and we in theirs. Billy and I often talked matter-of-factly about when we would marry, after we were all grown up. We planned to have lots of dogs and cats, French fries, and maybe kids. But, of course, as so often happens, life takes a few hard-to-anticipate turns along the way, and we lost touch before very long.

Wolf Clan

My first Native American 'happening' occurred at this country place. It would be many years before I realized the significance and importance of this event. From the time of my earliest memory, I loved any fur-bearing creature. The tactile sensation of running my fingers through a cat or dog's fur, of burying my face in their fur, was sheer pleasure to me. Ladies wore fur coats in those days and I recall my mother apologizing for my behavior to a startled lady whose fur coat I had been petting—while she was wearing it. Nothing of a furry nature was safe from me. Fluffy towels, sweaters, and long grass were also 'fair game.'

We didn't have a dog, so it was a delight to see Billy come strolling into our yard with his big black and white dog, Shep. I wanted to be with the dog every minute, and that is where I received my first, painful initiation into Wolf Clan society. This particular day, I was eating saltines while tightly hugging Shep about the neck with my free arm. Without warning, the dog suddenly attacked me. My mouth was open as I started to take another bite of crackers when the dog suddenly bit me in the face, his upper teeth on the outside of my right cheek, his lower teeth on the inside of my mouth. It was all over in an instant, but great damage had been done. His lower teeth had raked the soft tissue inside my cheek out, back to front. In fact, my mother said you could look right through my cheek and see my teeth. Fortunately, the skin had not been broken. Although there was no external scarring, there was so much scarring on the inside that, since that long-ago time, whenever I am nervous or cold, that scar tissue tightens, sometimes causing speech to be difficult. I screamed, blood streaming from my mouth, and the dog immediately let go. The dog was normally so good-natured and gentle everyone found it puzzling that he would suddenly bite anyone, especially a child. We later learned that the excitement of a chewing action in such close proximity had triggered an ancient feeding response, and hence the unfortunate incident.

I was quickly taken to see the doctor in a nearby small town. He soaked cotton balls in iodine and, using forceps, packed them into the wound. I remember crying out just before I fainted from the unbearable pain. The tragedy of the event was that the disease of rabies was on the rise in those days, and since so many cases in wild animals had been reported, the doctor insisted the dog be killed and examined at the state laboratory to determine if the disease was present. At the age of five, I pleaded with them not to do this. I said Shep could be penned up to see if he got the disease. The doctor told me that they weren't doing it to be cruel to the dog.

He spoke to me as though I were an adult, explaining that by the time symptoms appeared, it would be too late to treat me for the resultant Lockjaw and subsequent death that was usually inevitable. He said he needed to know as soon as possible, since the treatment at that time was a series of twenty-one shots given through the navel. Everyone said it was very painful. Still, I pleaded for Shep's life.

The pain I incurred as a result of my wound was nothing to how I suffered when I learned that my friend, Shep, had been killed. I was inconsolable then, and to this day, when something triggers a memory of those times, the unfairness of Shep's death, and my unwitting part in it, brings tears to my eyes.

I console myself with the thought that Shep gave his life so that I might become aware on some level that I was, indeed, related to those of his own kind through ancient symbiotic Wolf Clan medicine. Shep's bite had triggered within me collective memories of a time before, a time I harkened back to with each breath I took. But then, as so often happens in the framework of 'finding our way, seeking our true path, our Good Red Road,' over the course of time, "I forgot!" I forgot the very lessons that Shep had died to teach me. I forgot about the old days, and the old ways. I forgot about the spiritual interweaving of all things and all peoples. I later learned that, although "All Time *Is* All Time," there are frameworks within the workings of time that are not just the underpinnings, but are the true sub-structure in the *process* of time that impacts essential learning. And it was not yet time for me to learn. Five years would pass before another re-awakening occurred. At that time, the Shoshone Woman crossed to make her journey home.

The Poor Help the Poor

We lived at this country place for almost two years, and during that time, with the exception of the 'Shep initiation,' I have no recollection of any other extraordinary or psychic events occurring. I remember a carefree time, of running barefoot and wild, at play in the sunshine. I looked like a waif in those days, long-legged, colt-skinny, and tanned with unruly, fine, white blonde hair.

My brother and I went barefoot all summer. We were always on the move, exploring everything, 'into' everything. There were kittens in the barn to play with. We picked and ate wild blackberries in nearby berry patches and were mystified as to how our mother knew we had been in the woods. Mother taught us to help her in the garden, and we thought we were really important to be of help. We invented games and 'clubs' to belong to—a membership of two. We played ball and tag and hide and seek. We literally played outdoors from morning to night, and fell into bed each night relaxed and happy.

Our front yard faced onto a two-lane gravel road, our highway to the world! There was little traffic on this road, but whenever we heard a tractor, a farm vehicle, or an occasional car approaching, we called to one another and raced to the front yard to wave at the passersby.

Big open-bed trucks loaded with asparagus, corn, beans, and pumpkin, depending on the season, would frequently pass by, sometimes while my brother and I were playing in the front yard. These trucks were bound for the canning factory ten miles distant. Workers from Mexico, who tended the fields, rode on the produce trucks, and when they appeared, we would suspend play to stare in wide-eyed wonder at this rare traffic event. The workers were always laughing and talking; they waved to us in a friendly way. Often, they would carefully pitch bundles of asparagus or ears of corn to us, calling out for us to take these to our mother. In the fall of the year, from dawn to dusk, trucks heavily loaded with the perfectly ripened golden-orange pumpkins slowly made their way past our home headed for the cannery. Somehow, those workers managed to leave two perfect pumpkins, unbroken, at our home just before Halloween. For a day, they were Jack-O-Lanterns my brother and I delighted in; then, they were glorious pumpkin pies, thanks to our mother's culinary talent. Because of the generosity of these kind and jovial workers, my family enjoyed many fine meals. Years later, we realized they probably recognized our need and elected to help. I know a lot of people thought of our family as 'poor.' In retrospect, these kind and jovial strangers were very probably much less fortunate than us. My Mother once made the comment "the poor help the poor." So it would appear.

Fire Flies and Story Telling

We next moved to a very small town located on a major highway. This was exciting for us, as many vehicles went by all the time, and we sat by the hour on the steps of the small front porch watching traffic. In addition, two slippery, round, steel poles supported the roof on the porch. We continually climbed and slid down these poles. We imagined we were in the circus and felt quite daring. Across the street from us was a small tavern with a gas pump. Two doors down from us was another tavern. Across the street from us was a home that had been converted from the original, huge, old-time hotel. Across the street and up the way was a lumbering, old-fashioned two-story schoolhouse. Our parents kept a big garden, and just on the other side of the garden and some trees was a combination gas station/candy store. This was a child's dream! The lady who owned the store was called Missy S.

She had never married, and in those days was politely referred to as a spinster lady. It was rumored that she had suffered polio as a child, resulting in a slightly crippled leg. This was never mentioned, however, and she got about as best she could with a cane. She quickly 'adopted' my brother and me, as she had adopted all the children in the neighborhood as her extended family. We all loved her. She made ice cream cones for us, and when she dipped ice cream, it was all the ice cream you could get on one cone and still hold for a nickel! Some of the ice cream cones had 'free' slips of paper in the bottom of the cone. It seemed to us that we received an inordinate amount of free cones. It always seemed that the children were much luckier than their parents in receiving the free cones. Missy S. kept cats, all sorts of cats, and we thoroughly enjoyed playing with them, welcoming new kittens, and watching them at play around the store.

Directly across the street from our house was a tavern with a single gas pump. This tavern was a gathering place for the community, a place to drink and visit with friends, family, and acquaintances alike.

A square wooden table occupied a quiet corner of the room reserved for ongoing card games. The history of the table was forever etched into the wood, heavily scarred from cigar and cigarette burns and sporting eternal rings left by glasses used long ago. Countless dropped ashes and spilled drinks had changed the color of the wood over the course of time. Here and there was a scar in the table surface, suggesting a knife blade might have been stuck blade down, readily accessible to cut off a "chaw" of tobacco.

Kids and neighborhood dogs chased one another around the building, screaming and laughing. A big open lot behind the building was used for playing games—baseball, tag, leapfrog, and "Rover, Red Rover, Can You Come Over," to name a few.

A nondescript collection of outbuildings, including an outhouse, loosely encircled the main tavern building. The outhouse was surrounded by a bevy of hollyhocks in various colors, and afforded some extra privacy.

In mid-summer, fireflies seemed to magically appear each night just at dusk. All the children would chase them, and contests were held to see who could catch the most fireflies before letting them all go.

Sunset signified that it was time to play "Hide and Seek," a popular game, with the child who was 'it' flitting about, hiding in and around the outbuildings. When it became too dark to play outside, our parents would call us to come in. We willingly stopped playing because we knew we were in for a treat. Once indoors, we gathered quietly with snacks and drinks, and waited for Wild Tom to appear.

Wild Tom was a storyteller; he told stories in the tavern, at home, in the parking lot, anywhere he had an audience. He loved to tell stories, and we loved to hear those stories. Because our storyteller claimed to have known all the well-known outlaws and lawmen in the old-time western United States, he was called Wild Tom, by adults and children alike. I doubt anyone ever called him Wild Tom to his face, or in hearing of his family, but had he known, I imagine he would have been pleased at the title.

Everyone who knew Wild Tom jokingly referred to his 'selective hearing loss.' That meant that he could hear all women when they spoke to him, including his wife, but only when the mood struck him did he care to hear what men had to say. Wild Tom was definitely his own man, and lived, without apology or explanation, according to his own dictates.

Some of the adults were overheard to say that Wild Tom was just a 'big kid at heart.' Certainly he loved children, and, being quick and agile, he could often be seen joining in the children's games of tag or Hide and Seek. Wild Tom, though small of stature, was 'wiry' and, to all appearances, very strong for his size, easily lifting and carrying a keg or several cases of beer at a time.

Stories told by Wild Tom were often accompanied by the 'buzzing' of rattlesnake rattles palmed loosely in his hand. We were allowed to look at the rattles, but not to hold them or touch them. Wild Tom told us the snake had given their rattles to him alone, as a gift. He told us that if anyone else handled them, they would cease to rattle. He liked to sit, catching the breeze, rocking on his front porch with his wife, Miss Em, on a warm summer evening. As the dusk settled in, with a multitude of neighborhood children, along with a few adults, assembled on steps and porch railings, the talk invariably turned to 'the old days.' Fascinating tales about ghosts, or outlaws, or cowboys, were set forth in the hush of a spellbound audience. Wild Tom's favorite story, however, was how he met and courted Miss Em. After more than sixty years of marriage, Wild Tom was more in love with Miss Em than ever.

Whatever the story, and some of the favorites we heard again and again, we listened with baited breath, our hearts beating faster than usual, to tales of shootouts and life in mining camps, tales of stagecoaches, wolves and buffalo, hard winters, and trail drives. We heard about Mexicans, mountain men, Canadians, Indians, and Chinamen. We heard how the rails were laid down for the Iron Horse to travel on from city to city. We 'flew across the plains' with herds of wild horses. We trapped beaver and wintered in the high country. This was a whole new world to us, and it was such an exciting world that, many nights, we could not settle to sleep with the all the vivid, shadowy figures drifting in and out of our consciousness and dreams. It was all so real to us. We didn't realize it at the time, of course, but Wild Tom had laid the groundwork for a lifelong love of history, with the great humanizing elements of individual and collective peoples overlaying the vast panorama of life.

Every now and then, we children and Mother were invited to Wild Tom's home for 'a bite of lunch' at Miss Em's table. This was an eagerly awaited event, as Miss Em was a really good cook who loved to bake cookies and cakes and pies. Everything on the table was always homemade or from the garden. Having raised ten children, and entertaining a host of grandchildren and great grandchildren, Miss Em found it difficult to cook for just the two of them. She enjoyed cooking for company. Miss Em was a small, pretty woman, very gentle and fragile appearing in her ways. Sometimes, if she were home alone, we children would help her pick beans from her garden or sit on the porch and tip and tail the beans for her. At the end of every meal, Wild Tom would go to Miss Em, give her a kiss on the cheek, and turn to us, saying, "The first meal we ate as a married couple, I promised Miss Emily I'd thank her for every meal she ever cooked for me." And shy Miss Em would color up and flutter her apron a time or two, and say, "Now, Thomas." But you could tell she was really pleased. This unique man continued to honor his 'prairie bride' in this courtly manner, all the days of their lives together.

The Wages of War

During this time of new learning, it became apparent to my brother and me that all was not well in the home. My father was a carpenter. He worked hard and would come home from work, wash up, and, after 'supper,' adjourn to one of the neighborhood taverns to spend the rest of each evening. Most times, my mother stayed at home with us, since we were still just six and four years old. At the time, I had no idea that my dad was one of countless victims who had forever been maimed from their War experiences. From all accounts, Dad had entered the war as an idealistic, fun-loving guy. When he returned, he was often moody and, though reserved by nature, seemed to retreat even deeper within himself, sometimes more than others. Only drinking seemed to numb his senses enough to allow him respite from the demons of War, which forever tormented him.

Upon his return, Dad never talked about the War, and had no respect or tolerance for anyone who did. He entered the Army in January of 1942, a month after Pearl Harbor was bombed, and served in combat situations until the end of the war in 1945. Dad's military experience included serving under General George S. Patton in North Africa, where his was one of the first infantry units to engage the great German tank commander, General Erwin Rommel, in the Libyan dessert. Dad had tremendous respect for the courage and innovative tactics employed by General Rommel. He always felt that General Rommel was one of the greatest strategists to emerge from World War II. From Africa, Dad's unit went on to invade Sicily and Italy.

On very rare occasions, when he was especially inebriated, Dad would make reference to picking up and bagging enough body parts to weigh sixty pounds for reutrn to the United States for burial as someone's son, father, or brother. What was never talked about, however bespoke countless encounters with mindless, annihilating terror of such a magnitude as to drive any sensitive, sentient being to the brink of madness. It was no wonder to me that Dad self-medicated with alcohol. The wonder of it was that he, or anyone else, returned from War with even a shred of their former sanity.

The party atmosphere at War's end lent itself well to a drinking atmosphere. America had emerged from the Great Depression and had united to survive the most horrific war ever fought up to that time. Soldiers had returned to their families and business was 'booming.' The soldiers so recently returned from war balanced the joy of just being alive, and home with loved ones, against the bittersweet knowledge of friends forever lost and optimistic youth never to be recovered. They often experienced a kind of euphoria, but more often, felt adrift, out of place, out of sync for their place and time. The horrifying events that had for years made up the core fabric of their lives must have caused them to view 'ordinary' peacetime living as mundane and ludicrous beyond belief. The wives and children they loved, and were so happy to come home to, were strangers to them, living reminders of wistful, distant memories of earlier, happier times when the world stretched out in unending wonder and opportunity.

So they gathered to drink and smoke, to laugh and dance. The jukebox was never silent, and through the strident sounds of forced inebriated gaiety, the edges of darkness were pushed back for a few fleeting hours of poignant celebration. But things were forever changed, and gradually, perhaps in a vain attempt to regain those more innocent times, every night became a new and more frenzied 'New Year's Eve!'

Diverse Cultures

It was while we were living here that the gypsies came to town. My brother and I attended a country school located about a block from our house. The schoolhouse was an outsized, two-storied, boxy affair with huge windows and doors. Behind the school stretched a large grassy area where we played ball and all manner of sports and games. And one fine day, during the summer recess, that entire big, grassy field was suddenly and mysteriously filled, packed with impromptu rows of large trucks and cars pulling campers, or what were in those days called 'house-trailers.' These portable 'homes,' colorfully painted and decorated with a multitude of exotic designs, proved to be an unending topic of conversation to the entire community. Moreover, these were unusual looking folks. They all had olive-colored skin and dark, thick hair. Many of the men wore their hair long, but pulled back and neatly tied, and also wore gold earrings. The women wore full length, flounced print skirts and blouses, or dresses, accented by multitudes of colored glass bead necklaces. The amount of bracelets they wore on their wrists could not be counted. These exotically beautiful women, with their wild, long, dark hair, seemed always to be enjoying themselves, talking and laughing with one another, and all the while, their many bracelets tinkled gaily on their wrists as they moved their hands in graceful motion when speaking. The men wore white shirts, the sleeves rolled up tightly on their muscled biceps. They wore black boots and bright, fringed sashes about their waists. They were a darkly handsome lot, and seemed to be more serious than the ladies. All of them had the whitest teeth I had ever seen, and they smiled a lot. We did not understand their language, but they understood some of ours.

These folks often appeared at Missy S's store to shop for milk, bread, and other supplies. One day, I was helping my mother pull weeds in the garden, which was right next to the store. A little gypsy boy, with the brightest black eyes I had ever seen, stood barefoot in the shade of a tree, watching me in an alert, interested manner. He was in the process of eating a fast-melting ice cream cone, and seemed impervious to the drips falling onto his clothes as he watched me. I could not help but stare back at him. Abruptly, he flashed a big smile at me. I smiled back, a long-legged, tanned, tow-headed colt of a girl. The boy smiled at me once again, and was gone.

It happened that on another day, Mother and I were also out in the garden pulling weeds when I heard my mother suddenly scream and bolt out of the garden. Two Gypsy men were next door at the store, and one of them came over and, without a word, walked into the garden. He leaned down and, in a sudden movement, picked up a very large snake, about five or six feet long, by the tail. He looked at it briefly, shrugged apologetically, and, with a single movement, snapped it like a bullwhip, killing it instantly. He then tossed the snake into the road, nodded to my mother, and went on his way.

So this was the summer of the Gypsies, an introduction to my second alien culture. First, I had encountered the kind Mexicans, and now these equally solicitous Gypsies. For me, the world was expanding, and within a short time, I was to add to the list an African-American lady and a Native American gentleman.

The 'colored' lady, as African-Americans were called in those days, was a fragile, delicate, little lady, a widow who spoke softly in a low musical voice and just happened to be blind. I was, it was widely agreed, possessed by 'problem hair.' My hair was very fine, very soft, and was seemingly out of control at all times. I used to joke that I spent my whole childhood looking like a dandelion caught in the wind. It was a fair description. So one day, my Mother and a friend stopped to ask advice about my hair of the blind lady. My Mother pressed me forward in introduction, and the lady said, "Child, may I touch your face?" Having no experience in such matters, I nodded mutely, and my mother avowed as how it would be all right. The lady's small, cool fingers were as delicate as butterfly wings as she carefully felt of my face and smoothed a hand gently over my hair. Finally, she relaxed back into her rocking chair with a sigh.

"You are such a pretty child," she laughed, "but, honey, that hair is a caution!"

I didn't know what a caution was, but other adults in the room concurred with the lady's assessment.

"What do you think can be done?" my mother asked. "I tried giving her a permanent wave, but even that wouldn't take."

"Why don't you let me try French braiding her hair?" the lady asked.

"Isn't the hair too fine?" my mother inquired.

"No, ma'am, I believe I can do it," the lady answered.

This French braiding took a long time, but I was fairly mesmerized by watching the entire endeavor in a hand-held mirror. The hair was parted and clipped until it was time to braid that particular section, and the fine hair was tightly weaved into ever so tiny braids, which, in turn, were woven into other little braids. It actually felt very good on the scalp and, when it was done, there wasn't a single piece of 'fluff' to be seen. It looked to me as though I were wearing a wonderfully decorated cap that fit my head perfectly. It all looked neat and nice, and lasted nearly a day before the fine tendrils of hair began to work loose from the whole. Although this gentle soul and several generations of her people before her are, and had been, American citizens, I added her to my slowly expanding international culture base as an African-American. I will never forget this lady and the dignified, yet warmly cordial, manner in which she presented herself as our hostess.

An Old-Fashioned School

Grade school was a wonderful affair! All eight grades were gathered together in one big room with huge windows as the main source of study light. The 'biggest' kids, or eighth graders, were gathered to the far left of the great room, facing the blackboard. From left to right, the grades descended in age and numerical sequence, so that the youngest students were closest to the door, assuring quicker access to the privy, or 'outhouse,' should it be needed. Over the faded blackboard at the front of the school-room hung a series of pull-down 'maps of the world,' a never-ending source of wonder. The ABC's were carefully block-printed to the right side of the blackboard and, directly beneath, examples of both printing and cursive in both upper and lower case were expressed. I can recall carefully tracing the handwritten letters on the roof of my mouth – using my tongue as a pen.

For my seventh birthday present, I received a big, gold and white collie puppy. I named him Shep, in memory of the other Shep, who had initiated me into Wolf Clan ways. I spent a good portion of time each day playing with Shep, petting and grooming him. I was thrilled to be with him. Since my birthday is in June, I was able to spend the entire summer with him before returning to school in the fall. And when school was first in session, neither Shep nor I cared to be apart. Usually, Shep was in the yard, tied with a rope, but when I walked to school, Shep was put in the garage so he couldn't follow. He had other plans, however, and as soon as he could dig up the dirt floor of the garage and squeeze out, Shep, covered with dirt from his tunneling, would follow my scent into the school and trot directly to my desk, where he promptly laid down for the rest of the session and slept contentedly until school was out.

Those early school days were happy memories of ringing an old fashioned hand-held bell to signal that recess was over, erasing the blackboards at the end of the day and then taking the erasers outside to clap them together to get the chalk dust out, running and playing ball during recess, and Mrs. Goldie reading aloud to us such exciting tales as Rip Van Winkle. We also had tornado practice. Each of us was assigned to a 'big kid' who would be responsible for us if a tornado came. There was a cloakroom where one of the 'big' boys was responsible each day for seeing that a bucket of fresh water was pumped from a well and brought in. A big porcelain dipper was kept on a hook beside the water for anyone who cared to drink.

One bright autumn day, Mrs. Goldie took all of us up to the

second floor of the school building, and we were amazed at the treasure trove of old costumes and dusty scenery that we discovered there. All eyes were drawn to the front of the room, which had been fashioned into a makeshift stage with heavy faded red curtains stretched across one end of the room. The heavy curtains dipped precariously at the center, after many years of hanging immovable on the stressed wire upon which they hung. Nevertheless, there was a sense of aging grandeur about the whole scene, and all of us stood in awe at this representative spectacle of times past.

Mrs. Goldie then proceeded to open a box she had carried upstairs with her. In the box were two dozen kazoos. She informed us that we were going to put on an old fashioned minstrel show. None of us knew what a minstrel show was, so she was quick to explain. She asked one of the girls to bring a broom upstairs. Then we took turns sweeping up the dust and cobwebs from an area in front of the stage. When Mrs. Goldie was satisfied that it was clean enough, she asked us all to sit down on the floor, and there, with dust motes dancing on the rays of the filtered sunlight permeating the room, she told us about minstrel shows. She told us that in the old days, there were troupes of show folk, who would travel about the countryside, singing, dancing, and acting in 'skits,' or short plays, in 'black-face' (white actors rubbed burned cork onto their faces in order to 'blacken' their faces to play the part of black folks). We sat enthralled as Mrs. Goldie spoke in a quiet way about a part of our not-so-distant history, which we were to learn later on, involved racism and segregation. But in those days of first-grade innocence, proudly wearing my mother's kitchen curtains as a veil, I played the part of a young bride and, for a single magical night, I was transported into an exciting other-worldly realm of lantern-light and wonder, a world where time stood still. I look back upon that wonderful night as an end to childhood, the beginning of a new, more grown-up way of life.

My Howard

Many adult years had come and gone when I first met Howard on a tennis court. A group of us would meet every day and play impromptu matches, switching partners for doubles tennis, playing singles tennis, and every once in awhile, I was paired for a match with Howard. I thought he was a really good player, and we won our first match handily. After tennis, many of our group would adjourn to a local restaurant where we enjoyed a late brunch. In this way, I came to know him, but had no thoughts of a romantic nature about him.

As our friendship progressed, we gradually slipped into a relationship. Our second date involved flying less than an hour to a Florida location where we landed at a small airport, walked to a restaurant for wonderful hot fudge sundaes, and then continued on to a large building near the harbor where we attended a "Ditching At Sea" Seminar. It was fully dark when we began our flight home, and as we winged our way over the large city below, it looked like a fairyland with bright, twinkling, lights from horizon to horizon. As the lights of the city faded behind us, the sky took on a life of its own, expressed by stars and planets in a bright display against a dark sky. Gradually, I became aware that a small sliver of crescent moon was 'coming up.' The night became a creature of its own making, gloriously insular, safe, in the sweet purr of the plane's engine.

Some of our tennis friends who had flown with Howard advised me that he took unnecessary chances in the air. I felt sure they were exaggerating. As I was soon to learn, he was not a big fan of the 'straight and level' school of flight mindset. Later, when Howard began to teach me the principals of flight, I soon came to realize that, though he might take calculated risks, Howard *always* made sure the percentages were on his side.

Our *first* date was unbelievable. One day, Howard asked if I would like to take a ride in his airplane. I leaped at the chance. He picked me up at my home and we drove out to a grass-covered landing strip in the 'middle of nowhere.' When we stepped out of the car, cows were grazing around the plane. "Watch where you step," Howard cautioned. As Howard walked me through the pre-flight check, the cows gradually munched their way 'elsewhere.' Howard asked me to leave my purse in his car, which I thought was a bit unusual. He climbed under a wing, opened a valve to allow a small stream of fuel to drain into a clear container, and then carefully checked the fuel for condensation. Finding none, he carefully stowed the testing cup away in the car, along with a few other things from a ledge over the rear seat of the plane. In retrospect, this should have been a clue to me, but I had no idea who I was dealing with at the time—just a very nice man, I thought.

After carefully checking out and untying the plane, Howard told me to get in the cockpit to 'prime' the plane while he turned the prop by hand. I did, though not without some reservations. Checking the wind with a wet finger, he climbed into the plane and started up the engine. He explained to me that the engine needed a bit of time to warm up. While the engine was warming up, Howard explained the purpose of each instrument, showed me how to use the radio, including how to declare an emergency. Finally, he taxied to the end of the runway for takeoff. The runway looked very short to me. Two forested areas of seventy- to one-hundred-foot trees were prominent at each end of the runway. I worried aloud that the cows might run out in front of the plane at the last minute. Howard laughed at me, told me to belt in firmly, and to keep my left arm in close to my body. I quickly learned the logic of this. He taxied full tilt toward the tall trees at the end of the runway and, all at once, we were airborne. Without warning, Howard suddenly jerked a metal bar between the seats up, and I heard a loud snap. This, I was later to learn, was the sound made as Howard retracted the manual landing gear. I further learned that it was Howard's general practice to retract the gear once fifteen feet of air space separated the plane from the ground! All at once, the plane sank so that we were racing at an incredible speed (or so it seemed), only about ten feet off the ground, towards trees that loomed over us with a menacing attitude. With the increased aerodynamics caused by tucking the wheels into the fuselage, air speed was dramatically increased, and, without warning, the plane veered up sharply and banked to the left. We began climbing. Seeing that I was somewhat shaken by what I perceived to be a near-death experience, Howard kindly reassured me that once the gear is retracted, the plane always sinks momentarily, but is then able to build up even more speed. "If you have enough speed and enough altitude, you can do anything," he laughed. I was shortly to discover the truth of this statement—in a variety of distressing ways. I did not know it then, but my life, once again, would never again be the same.

I was fairly glued to my window, excitedly looking at the view etched sharply in such sun-lit detail it caused the eyes to hurt. The tiny little houses, even smaller cars, and miniscule cows browsing in pastures cut through with meandering creeks offered a perspective new to me. I had flown only twice before, and found this to be a completely natural, thrilling, wonderful world. As we gradually worked our way to the two-mile high altitude, I couldn't help but be enthralled by the green corn fields standing out in stark delineation right next to a golden wheat field, which, in turn, lay next to a newly plowed field, ready for planting.

Thus absorbed in the view, I was surprised when Howard directed the plane into a nearly straight-up maneuver, and heard the engine sputtering to a complete stop. Without warning, Howard kicked in a hard left rudder and the plane began screaming straight down toward the ground. This seemed to go on forever in slow motion. I felt sure we were not going to be able to pull out of this horrendous dive, but I was almost too nauseated to care. At the last minute, or so I thought at the time, Howard pulled back on the control yoke and deftly steered us into a giant, slow loop. All at once, we were flying straight and level. Howard flashed me a quick grin and said, "How did you like that?" Fighting hard not to throw up, I said, "That was so much fun, I don't know why we didn't think of it before." And from that day forward to the day he died, Howard and I were a matched set. We lived together, and loved together, and more times than I can count, we trusted our very lives to one another. There was only one Howard, and I count myself the luckiest person alive to have been his wife. Together, we were larger than life.

Between Sea and Sky

I later learned that when he was seven years of age, Howard 'built' his first sailboat from a modified rowboat that he converted to a sailing dinghy, and hauled it on his little red wagon to a nearby bay where he launched it and immediately set sail. From that day forward, he was a creature of the sea. The sea called to him throughout his life and, until the end, he was never without a boat or boats. A week before he crossed, Howard sailed into the Gulf of Mexico with his all-girl crew, as he expressed it. He was greatly weakened by Leukemia at that time, and was bundled up against the rawness of the brisk, breezy day. Howard directed his granddaughter, daughters, grandson's fiancè and me as to setting our course, trimming the sails, and handling the helm, while he and his grandson enjoyed a relaxed visit. Howard always loved to sail 'hard to the wind,' or 'close to the wind,' and no matter how fierce was the blowing wind, he consistently threw up every sail he had. Sailing speed is obtained by gathering into your sails as much wind as possible, while, at the same time, keeping as much of your hull length in the water as possible; in short, not heeling too far over.

Howard told me once he was born to fly, and I believe it! He said that he always knew he could fly. He felt he was a 'natural born pilot.' And so he was. Howard suffered one of the great disappointments of his life when, because of a mild color-blindness, he failed to be accepted into flight school in the Second World War. I feel sure he could have become an Ace!

After the War, Howard graduated from college with a degree in Physics. He married, and he and his wife were blessed with three daughters. His family, his sister's family, and their parents lived in the Long Island, New York community where he had grown up. With his family and life-long friends close by, Howard's life seemed perfect. His passion for flying never abated and he eventually bought a seaplane. At that time, Howard was unlicensed and working with only rudimentary instruction volunteered by the previous owner of the plane. Naturally, he set forth to teach himself to fly. He kept his plane tied to a mooring behind his home on the bay, and, whenever he had a few moments free, he would loose the moorings and taxi the plane out to sea, until one day when, facing into the wind, he developed enough power to achieve liftoff. From that day forward, he was a great seat-of-the-pants pilot. He later bought a high performance, variable pitch propeller aircraft, a Mooney, and, achieving his instrument rating, ranged out in his flights until he had literally flown from Alaska to Trinidad. At the time when he flew to Alaska, he didn't yet have his instrument rating, and relied instead on his good judgment, great navigating ability, and the kindness of fate. I used to say that Howard lived under a lucky star, and so he did. He often found himself in dangerous, even life-threatening, situations, but he, himself, failed to perceive them as a threat, and so, to him, they were 'no problem.'

Adventuring

Howard and I had been together twelve years, both as a committed live-in couple and then as a married couple. These were glorious years of personal growth and expansion, years of exploration and travel, years of family and fun. They were also years of frustration, confusion, and, on occasion, anger. But that is growth. No growth can occur without some pain resulting from the expansion process. Overall, however, our marriage was an ongoing, ever-changing, loving celebration of life and one another.

Though I had always enjoyed an inborn sense of adventure coursing through every fiber of my being, that sense of adventure was never fully explored until I met Howard. His love of adventure was the cornerstone of his being. He was an adventurer of the highest order. I used to wonder if Howard ever experienced fear in any way. I came to realize that he didn't dwell on fear or negatives, but instead concentrated on 'giving himself the best odds possible,' which still equated to 'over the top' danger for most people.

Over the course of our time together, we sailed thousands of miles, flew many more thousands of miles, and motor-homed extensively. Whenever we went on vacation, it wasn't for a week or two—it was for months on end. Although we visited big cities, and enjoyed them, the major part of our traveling was in complete wilderness situations, which we both loved.

Looking back, I think Howard's greatest gift to me was to suddenly throw me into situations I didn't feel capable of handling, and then insist that I handle them anyway. One such event occurred when we had pulled anchor to head out of Norfolk Harbor, back out to sea, as we continued to sail north up the Atlantic seaboard. Howard advised me to take the helm while he went below to chart our course as we headed into Hampton Roads. He had only been below a few minutes when I became jarringly aware that two huge vessels returning from the Atlantic were approaching The Lady Grace head-on.

Panicking, I yelled below, "Howard, there's an aircraft carrier and a nuclear submarine cruising on the surface headed directly for us. Please—come take the helm!"

"Sorry, Baby, I can't leave these charts," his voice floated up from below.

"What!" I couldn't believe my ears.

"I said, 'I can't leave these charts.'"

Blood pounding in my ears, I shouted, "Well, what should I do?"

Unbelievably, a note of amusement in his voice, my husband called up to me, "Don't hit them."

There was no time to argue, no time to plead my case. I knew that I was to be given no quarter, and that the future of our lives depended on the decisions I now made. Each of these huge vessels, virtually abreast of one another, was bearing down on our thirty-four-foot sailboat at an alarming speed, or so it seemed to me. I remembered one of the first instructions Howard had given me on how to direct your course when meeting another boat. He said that while most vessels meet port to port, just as cars in the United States do, on the sea, what really matters is that you commit to a course as early as possible and ascertain that the other captain understands your actions. My assessment of the immediate situation we faced was that if I stayed the course, I would indeed pass the carrier port to port and, recognizing I had no time to move to Starboard to put the nuclear submarine on my port side, as well, I elected to hold my course, straight on, and "split the herd"—not a well known sea term, by the way.

Long minutes passed as I sailed between the two vessels. It seemed to me that time had stopped, and was standing still, that I would forever be attempting to hold a steady course between these two behemoths of the sea.

The reality of time was brought home to me in a rush as

hundreds of sailors on the carrier, decked out in their dress whites, began waving and cheering as I came in the lee of the carrier. It was only then that I realized how they perceived the situation, most probably after being months at sea; below them was a tanned blond wearing a bright pink bikini, apparently alone on this sleek sailboat. I blushed to the roots of my hair, though I'm sure no one could see that.

Keeping a close eye on the nuclear submarine, so as not to sail too close, I perceived that the men aboard the sub were much more subdued. Some men were topside, obviously officers, and seemed to be 'all business.' There were no greetings, no waves or smiles as I sailed safely past the huge vessel.

My husband appeared from below, grinning at me. "Well done," he said as he took the helm. "Let's strike the sails and put in. I'm taking you out to dinner."

It was such a relief to put into port after my 'harrowing ordeal.' Food never tasted so good. After dinner, our dog, Tippy, joined us in an evening walk as the last golden rays of the setting sun cast a glowing 'net' over all. And the wind was strengthening.

This was just one of many times to come in which I was to celebrate my husband's great gift, not only to me, but to nearly everyone he met. He had the rare ability to challenge you in such a way that you were forced to 'go beyond yourself,' to become more than you had been. Once the dangers involved were past, and I realized I was still alive, a sense of euphoria always set in, accompanied by a sense of pride as I realized that I had grown and become more, a new, stronger, braver, more savvy person, capable of meeting new and unusual situations and challenges. I had been 'put to the test' by the husband who loved me, had lived to tell the tale, and the strength of character brought about by this testing became a part of me forevermore. Thank you, my beloved. Thank you, my Howard.

The Last Christmas

The Last Christmas for my husband proved to be a unique and powerful spiritual experience. Christmas was Howard's favorite holiday and, with that in mind, I had decorated each and every room of our home with small trees, strung with lights and ornaments; favorite Christmas candles, and cards from friends taped around doorways and on mirrors. Until the last two days of his life, Howard had 'held court' in our living room, stretched out on the couch, receiving visitors, watching television, and napping from time to time. It was a gathering place for Howard's sister, my mother, and me. Very often, we sat quietly, each reverting to personal thoughts, but most often we found ourselves engaged in pleasant, low-key conversation; Howard often joined in, but when he didn't feel well enough, he seemed quite content just listening to the light banter and recounting of family stories. As Howard gradually grew weaker, I realized that, at some point in time, he would probably be more comfortable in bed. Armed with this realization, I concentrated far more than usual on decorating our bedroom for Christmas. I wanted everything to be light, soothing, and festive. I wanted the feeling of Christmas to be alive with hope and reassurance. So I began with small brightly colored strands of Christmas lights, stringing them up all along the big double windows, single windows, and doors to the room. Our bed was positioned diagonally with an octagon shaped table behind it. The room was spacious enough to accommodate two sizeable dressers, two big chairs, two tables, and various mirrors and paintings. The way Howard rested in bed, his view was of a large painting of boats anchored and secured to docks and moorings in a harbor such as you might see in Maine. The wooden boats were from the 1930s and 1940s, the time when Howard was a youth. From where Howard lay in bed, he could also see the fifteen-inch ceramic Christmas tree I had put on top of the bookcase near the bed. I had also taped to the side of the bookcase Christmas cards that had arrived from friends, and had found many 'flying' and 'boating' Christmas cards to add to the mix, taping them up in an easy-to-see spot on the bookcase. A framed picture of Howard's beloved Mooney aircraft while he flew above Long Island Sound was clearly visible from where he lay. He seemed to be without pain, alternately dozing lightly and awakening just as quietly. Sitting near him, I would come to realize he had awakened and was gently smiling at me.

Throughout Howard's final month at home, our loving companion dog, Tippy, seldom left his side, going out only briefly to relieve himself, drink, or eat a little. Tippy seemed to understand that physical touch to Howard was painful. Now and again, Tippy would carefully work his head under Howard's hand in a gentle and encouraging way.

Howard had asked me to call his sister, Janelle, and my mother, Hazel, to come and be with us. Besides Tippy and me, Janelle and Mother were the only two people Howard wanted with him. And so we lived in gentle, uplifting harmony, loving and supporting one another, without false illusions and without trepidation, drifting on the gauzy winds of time.

When in the bedroom, Janelle, Mother, Tippy, and I would just sit quietly, the room lit only by the calm serenity of Christmas lights and the light of the small butterflies, birds and ornaments on the ceramic tree. On the day before he crossed, Howard awakened to this scene and sort of laughed, saying to me, "Why are you looking at me?" I grinned back and said, "Because it's my turn." We all chuckled.

Howard and I were in the uniquely lucky position of spending all our time together, and were hardly ever apart during our twelve years. I had always wanted to live 'hand-in-glove' with my special man, and this way of living was a great joy to me. Though his pain didn't allow for touching, we slept together, even on this, his last night with me. I was careful to move very quietly so as not to disturb him. We held hands and spoke together, and, not speaking, shed silent tears together for the loss we both knew was approaching. And Tippy rested his head quietly on the bed near Howard's right hand.

Howard slept deeply much of the next day. Occasionally, he would suddenly awaken, fully alert, and, in a strong voice, would ask, "What time is it?" After this had occurred a few times, Janelle said, "Why? Do you have a hot date?" Howard just laughed.

From the bedroom, I could hear Mother just starting supper and I could hear Janelle talking on the phone in the kitchen when Howard roused and asked me the time. Tippy was resting quietly on the floor, head between paws, close to Howard, near the head of the bed. I crossed the room to look at the clock in the dim light and returned to a place where Howard could easily see me, taking care not to step on Tippy. "It's six o'clock," I said. "Six o'clock at night?" Howard questioned. "Yes," I reassured him. All at once, he became restless, shifted around a bit, and said in a very distressed way, "Babe, the pain. I can't stand the pain." I quickly moved to his side as Howard suddenly, purposefully, propped himself up on his right elbow and looked straight up. All at once, he became quiet, staring raptly at the ceiling, the pain forgotten and the most beautiful smile spread clear across his face. It suffused his whole being with such an astonished look of absolute, pure, joyous recognition and reunion. He broke his skyward gaze for the briefest moment, looked at me with a small, apologetic, little-boy grin, brimming with love, but almost instantaneously, irresistibly, was drawn once again to look skyward in joy. I seemed to hear my own voice from afar, quietly confident, knowing. I felt a tremendous outpouring of love as I said to my husband, "Let go, Babe. It's OK. Just let go." And just as he had lived his entire life, with courage and conviction for a good outcome, without hesitation, Howard leaped, once more, into the unknown, eager at the chance for further adventure.

Howard had crossed. He was gone. I was unable to grasp the concept. I felt myself adrift in time with nothing to tie me to the

Earth when I became aware of a wet nose being eased under my hand and was brought back to 'reality.' I quickly sank to my knees and wrapped my arms around Tippy, hugging him closely to me, rocking back and forth. Without turning, I 'saw' Janelle and Mother come into the room, come up behind me, and put their arms around me. I still felt as if I were floating. The room seemed strangely the same, the same as 'before,' peaceful and serenely lighted by the cheerful colors of the small Christmas lights, which, through my tears, seemed like starbursts of light, strong and reassuring. In my 'mind's eye,' I saw Howard, steady at the helm, slicing through a crisp and frothy sea, sailing 'hard to the wind.' When last seen, Howard was confidently making with all possible haste for uncharted waters.

Adrift in an Alternate Universe

The time following a loved one's crossing might be compared to living in an alternate universe; at least, that's the way it was for me. My sister-in-law and my mother sustained me through Howard's final days. They remained with me for a week or so following Howard's memorial service. My brother and sister came from Colorado as soon as possible and a boyhood friend of Howard's surprised us by arriving unexpectedly. He had come quite a distance to say goodbye to his dear friend. With children in school, my sister arrived after the funeral, but was able to stay a week. All of these loved ones proved to be a great source of strength and comfort to me. When I look back on that time, though, I am aware that my reactions were 'off the charts.' I over-responded or under-responded to the slightest provocation, or to no provocation at all. Mother and Janelle assured me that my reactions were perfectly normal, 'under the circumstances,' and that 'things would get back to normal' at some point in time. I was not at all convinced.

An overall sense of brittle calm and pervasive cheerfulness seemed to overlay every aspect of our daily living. A strange sense of calm purpose suffused our lives. I seemed to be living outside myself, watching with subdued interest the preparations for my husband's service. I came out of my reverie from time to time, just long enough to oversee the details of Howard's service; after all, everything must be absolutely right.

My husband's daughters arrived a few days before the memorial service, in which they played such a major part. They were a great comfort and, in their usual resourceful way, just took charge of everything. They cooked, they cleaned, and they bolstered the morale of everyone. They helped plan the memorial service, helped to pick out pictures for the service, and ordered flowers. Together, they wrote the eulogy for Howard's service, and together, they delivered the eulogy.

Howard would have been so proud of his girls. They stood together, without tears, only occasionally pausing to regain their composure. Briefly, the girls outlined the story of their dad's life, citing funny and loving stories to remember the wonderful, moral, responsible man who had played a major part in rearing them to be such strong, compassionate, fun-loving, and able women. One of Howard's favorite sayings was "stop the nonsense." Each of us had heard the phrase on more than one occasion, usually in conjunction with some point Howard was trying to get across and found us resistant to. Following his death, when one of us would begin to cry, someone else would supply a comforting arm, and softly intone, "stop the nonsense." Of course there were times when we enjoyed a group hug and indulged in a group cry. Howard felt there was nothing his girls could not accomplish if they simply applied themselves, and they continued to live up to his trust and belief in them on all occasions.

As I sat quietly struggling for control over my emotions in the church pew, the priest began to speak, and I thought back to just a few days before when the priest, at Howard's request, had come to the house to talk with him. Mother, Janelle, and I initially gave the men privacy, wrongly assuming that deeply, confidential, serious discussions concerning the hereafter and the welfare of the immortal soul would take place.

Nothing could have been further from the truth. Howard and the priest chatted together like long lost buddies, about everything except the hereafter and the welfare of the immortal soul. Quite a lot of hilarity ensued on both sides with a barrage of joke telling, boating stories, and sharing of real life family fun. Finally, after sharing coffee, cookies, conversation, and a nice visit with all of us, the priest took his leave.

Later, in private, I said to my husband, "It sounded like you guys were laughing and talking non-stop. Did you discuss anything serious?"

"No, nothing serious," he said.

"I thought you might have issues he could help with."

Howard smiled. "Look, Baby," he said. "He's a man. I'm a man. We were both in the military. We both know what's going on. We understand each other. There's nothing to discuss."

I must have looked distressed. Howard took my hand. "There's nothing to worry about. Everything's OK."

"That priest is a heck of a nice guy," Howard added. "I want him to do my memorial service."

And so he did, and I found myself one unbelievable, surreal day, sitting among saddened friends, loving family, and supportive neighbors, listening to the comforting words of this Man of God who had discovered in my husband, ever-so-briefly, a fellow brother-at-arms.

Abruptly, the service was over, and we found ourselves in the bright sunlight, grouped on the steps of this beautiful, historic church for a photograph. At the time, I thought this a little disconcerting, but later took great comfort in looking at these pictures.

Everyone had been invited to come back to the house for refreshments. My brother was driving my car. From the passenger seat, I saw the funeral director coming down the steps of the church carrying the beautiful wooden box holding Howard's ashes. I called out to the funeral director, "Can Howard ride with us?"

A stunned silence ensued. Quickly regaining his composure, the funeral director called out, "of course." He then opened the passenger side door, and carefully handed the beautiful wooden box in to me. I felt vastly comforted. I felt Howard was smiling or laughing out loud.

My brother grinned at me. "Ready?" he asked.

"Yes, I'm ready. Everything's okay now. We're going home."

The gathering following the service was a joyous celebration of a life well lived, a tribute to the courage of the human spirit. Truly, my husband was a man who led by example. He knew how to live. And he knew how to die.

Personally, I can imagine no greater honor than to have been Howard's wife.

Within a couple of days, the girls had to leave to return to their jobs and their husbands. They were such a wonderful comfort to me, and their dad would have been so proud of the way they "stepped up to the plate."

Life After Howard

Living without Howard was unthinkable, unfathomable. How could he be gone? How could this be? For a time, in spite of the best help friends and family were able to offer, I was simply lost, adrift. In an effort to deal with the great void left in my life by Howard's crossing, I totally immersed myself in projects. I kept busy every single minute of the day. My plan was to leave no time for feeling sorry for myself. I was the queen of cheerful busy work. I was the queen of role-playing your way to success. Or so I thought.

I didn't know it at the time, but I was grieving deeply. So, too, was Tippy, our dog. Day wrapped into intolerable day, night into sleepless night. I didn't eat. I didn't sleep. I felt unsettled, unwell. But, in spite of my pain, I became aware that I felt better when I was outdoors in the fresh air. So Tippy and I began to spend a lot of time out of doors. He lay beside me wherever I was at work. I spent hours cleaning weeds from flower beds, planting flowers, trimming hedges, mowing the lawn, etc., and one day, I realized with a start, that I was enjoying myself.

Later, when my entire focus was simply to walk the Good Red Road, to live into the ways and truth of The Old Ones, I came to realize that, through my collective memories, I had been led to exactly the healing I so badly needed through touching our Mother, the Earth.

The year following Howard's crossing was a revelation—in so many ways. One of the more unpleasant revelations I referred to in my mind as 'Murphy's Law for Widows.' Truly, everything that could go wrong did go wrong! Wiring, plumbing, and air conditioning, to name a few of the problems I encountered, were all in need of attention. So I was kept busy with a host of kindly, patient workmen. I was left to assume that Howard had mysteriously maintained the home without my ever being aware of it. I have since learned from talking with other widows that each of them has encountered that 'first year' barrage of breakdowns and replacement needs. The thought has crossed my mind that maybe this is God's way of keeping us so busy that we don't have too much time to dwell on our loss. Whatever the reason, every single widow I have spoken with has encountered a similar situation.

In truth, many of the projects I worked on had been in need of attention for years, but had simply fallen by the wayside while Howard and I enjoyed our time traveling eight or nine months of the year. Even when we found ourselves at home, not a day passed that we didn't play tennis or golf, take a trip somewhere, or do some day sailing or flying. In addition, we made short trips to visit friends and family, and they reciprocated. Our home was always filled with love and laughter. Our life was a whirlwind of enjoyment and excitement. I am grateful for every single minute of that time.

I was unable to sleep at night and found myself reading until three or four in the morning. Most of my adult life, I have arisen at five o'clock in the morning. I consider this my personal quiet time, which I use to meditate, pray, read, or to catch up on correspondence.

It has always been my habit when the weather is fit to find myself sitting outdoors, enjoying the cool morning air, sometimes wrapped in a blanket. Dog curled contentedly at my feet, I mentally wrap myself in a cloak of celebration for the birth of a new day, a day in which anything could happen. Hands cupped around my coffee mug, the small one and I listen together to the sounds of birds joining in a cacophony of celebration. Before long, Grandfather Sun slowly shows himself and warms Mother Earth with his smile. My companion and I witness this glorious renewal, I like to say, through the process of 'osmosis.' And so we begin our day, reassured by witnessing, yet again, one more miracle! This tradition of joyous validation has always bolstered my morale, sustaining me in the best of times and the worst of times. Howard and I shared countless mornings together in this way.

Howard's wish was to be cremated. For nearly nine months following his crossing, I honored Howard's memory by setting up a personal altar. This memorial consisted of the simple, elegant, lustrous wooden box containing his ashes, along with a picture of Howard, in uniform, as a very young World War II Merchant Marine. An ongoing procession of fresh flowers graced a small bud vase during this entire time.

I spoke with my mother, who lived a thousand miles away, by phone at least once a day, and often three or four times a day. She was such a positive support during this time of recovery. She mentioned to me one day that she thought the memorial altar might act as an ongoing catalyst for depression or, at the least, might prolong my grieving process. I had not thought myself to be in a depressive state, but when I 'turned it over in my mind,' I wasn't so sure. I realized that if I were, indeed, depressed, I might not be able to recognize it myself.

Grief, for each of us, is such a nebulous concept. Someone once asked me, "How long does the grieving process take?" My reply to them was "It takes as long as it takes." I continued to honor my husband by memorial until the time for grieving was ended. At that time, I traveled with Howard's ashes to a place in the North, where his ashes were interred in a gravesite service, which included a military honor guard.

Janelle was concerned that, in suffering my loss, through a misguided sense of loyalty and love, I might join the ranks of those who have remained locked into memories of the past, so emotionally crippled that going forward was not an option. I have never forgotten her encouragement to me when she said, "You will always remember the love you enjoyed with Howard. You will never lose your memories, but it's time to move on now. Your life is like the chapters of a book. Each of the chapters provides us with the wisdom and knowledge that help to make us the person we are today. Some of the chapters seem more important and meaningful than others. This is not the case, however; each chapter is equally important and meaningful, no matter the lesson(s) that are gained. You move through one chapter; that chapter ends, and you go forward to begin another chapter."

Janelle's words continued to ring in my ears, and to this day, I find her advice caring, eloquent, and timeless in application. And so, I began, as I had done numerous times in many previous "chapters," to remake my life! As time passed, and as my sorrow eased somewhat, I decided I needed to set some short-term and long-term goals.

My short-term goal was to get a job. I had always worked as a secretary or librarian, and was fortunate enough to gain an entry-level position as a part-time secretary/receptionist at the church I attended. The job was very good for me. It became necessary for me to get up, shower, and put on a dress and high-heeled shoes to be appropriately presentable in my job. Through the church, I gradually became more involved in the community, meeting new friends, and making the acquaintance of other church secretaries in the community, who also became friends.

Following Howard's crossing, I relied heavily upon the love, loyalty, acceptance, understanding, and friendly support of my constant companion, Tippy, who had been with Howard and me since he was just six weeks old, a black and white bundle of puppy love and energy.

Tippy and I traveled everywhere together in the car, but he

was advanced enough in years that he no longer cared to accompany me on my brisk morning and evening walks. I did, however, drive him up to the park for a gentle stroll each day, where we walked out on the long fishing pier and enjoyed the grounds together.

I had an hour for lunch each day, and since I was only a five-minute drive from work, I came home to enjoy my lunch with Tippy and put my feet up for a few minutes. Evenings, we often sat side by side on the floor in the living room, watching TV, until time to go to bed. We fell into a pleasant, comfortable routine. Tippy gave my life purpose, and I didn't feel so lonely.

I met new friends. I took an evening computer course up at the high school and met not just my next-door neighbor lady there, but a 'new' lady friend, as well. The three of us started coming back to my house for a snack following classes. It turned out all three of us lived within a block of one another. Our friendship continues to this day.

Through my job at church, I met a tennis friend. I had not played for years, but always loved the game, and before long, my new lady friend and I were playing not only locally, but we traveled to other places to compete, as well.

I had joined a Bible Study group that met each Wednesday at the priest's residence and thoroughly enjoyed the lively, in-depth discussions that ensued. These studies were always followed by a community meal. It was about this time that I was asked to join a ladies group from Church. One of the members of the group was an elderly lady who, in spite of being nearly blind, was lively, pleasant, and in possession of a brilliant mind. She had been a schoolteacher. And, unbeknownst to me, she was the Mother of the Shaman. So the Shaman came into my life in an unusual way. Of course!

The Shaman Performs a Healing

My life seemed to be 'on track.' I felt I was successfully adjusting to being a family of one, as I put it. I was happy in my job, which continued to offer limitless challenges and opportunities for personal growth. I was in constant touch with my family and friends. Everything was fine—that is, until I had a major Crohn's Disease flare-up. The flare-up manifested itself in internal, breakthrough bleeding. I was already taking anti-inflammatory medication for my condition. To those drugs, my doctor added a strong-dosage steroidal drug. But the bleeding continued unabated.

Six weeks passed with no relief. I was exhausted all the time. I had quit playing tennis. I was barely able to drag myself out of bed to go to work each morning. Most evenings, when I got off work, I stopped at the grocery store to pick up deli or an already-prepared food product I could eat quickly and then fall into bed until the next morning. I was in a tough spot, and I knew it. I was keenly aware that if this problem were not quickly resolved, I would end up in the hospital with part of my digestive tract being removed. I was determined to avoid surgery at all costs.

One day, I was telling my elderly lady friend about my situation. She spoke up in a sprightly manner and said, "Why don't you go see my son? He's a Shaman, you know. He can heal you."

At this time in my life, I had no idea who or what a Shaman might be. Vaguely, I seemed to recollect that a Shaman was a holy man. It didn't really matter. I was desperate, so I said, "Would he see me?"

"Certainly," she replied.

"And would you stay with me for the healing?"

"I will certainly stay with you for the ceremony." Later on, I was to learn this was the only healing that she had ever actually attended, though her son occasionally confided in her about the people he was 'working with.'

That evening, I arrived at the home, nervous and exhausted, but filled with hope. As I got out of my car, I couldn't help but admire the first and second floors of this graceful home. Each floor showcased huge shaded 'decks,' set with French doors, which, remarkably, had been designed and built around huge old oak trees. I later learned that the Shaman was a builder by trade.

I greeted the mother, my friend. "Go right up," she said. "He likes to talk to folks beforehand. I'll be up in a little while."

The mother and son lived in a huge home; she lived on the ground floor, and he on the second floor. Arduously, I climbed the stairs to the second floor and rapped timidly on his door.

Abruptly, the door swung inward to reveal a huge man smiling in welcome. "Please—come in," he said pleasantly. As I stepped through the door, directly across from me was a nearly life-sized painting. My heart almost stopped. I couldn't catch my breath. I came close to fainting.

"What's the matter?" my host asked.

"That painting," I said weakly, pointing to a portrait of the Medicine Man who had come into my hospital room to save my life so many years before. "I know that man. He saved my life."

The Shaman smiled. "Mine, too," he said as he gently assisted me to a chair.

As the Shaman made small talk to put me at my ease, I gradually became aware that every inch of this huge great-room, with its vaulted ceiling, not taken up by windows, was graced by a vast multitude of paintings, mostly portraits, devoted to Native Americans. The eyes of the people depicted seemed to follow me everywhere. I was suffused with such a powerful feeling of joy and recognition, a feeling of 'coming home,' that tears spilled from my eyes.

The Shaman nodded approvingly. "What you are experiencing is a true connection to Spirit," he explained. "These are Spirit paintings."

He brought me a glass of water and said, "I hear you've been experiencing some internal bleeding. What do you think is causing this?"

"I really don't know," I said. "My whole life has been in chaos for nearly a year now, ever since my husband crossed. I have been struggling with my husband's loss, and working to settle his estate. I have had to repair so many things at the house—plumbing and electrical problems. I've been out of the workforce for over twenty years, but recently found a job I enjoy. It requires computer skills, so I am learning how to use the computer as I go, sort of on-the-job training! I miss my husband a lot, but I'm doing the best I can. Who knows? Maybe all this stress is just catching up to me."

"Maybe," he volunteered. "We'll see."

I was surprised by the sudden realization that although this man was a perfect stranger to me, I felt completely at ease. I trusted him implicitly. As though reading my mind, he smiled. "Let me tell you a little bit about myself, and about the ceremony that will commence in a few minutes." Again, as though reading my mind, he said, "Mom will join us shortly. I'll call her on the phone when it's time to come up."

"I serve as a Hollow Bones for the Old Ones," he continued. "The Old Ones pour their healing energy through me into the one being healed. I guess you could say I am like a conduit for energy transfer."

"We will begin by saying prayers and, with Great Creator's approval, a healing circle will be formed. The Grandfathers and Grandmothers will take their places in the circle, and we will begin."

"They tell me this healing will be to rid you of grief, to rid you of wrongly-assumed guilt in the care and treatment of your husband. The Old Ones want you to know it is normal to think that you didn't do enough for your loved one, or that you did too much, or that you made wrong decisions about his care. You need to let go of these negative thoughts. You are a human being, and human beings make mistakes; that is how we learn. I feel certain your husband had no complaints. Be assured that your husband not only forgives you for any wrongs you assume responsibility for, but he loves you more today than the first time he realized he was in love with you. You need to find a way to forgive yourself. You are assuming blame for situations and circumstances over which you had no control."

I was struggling to absorb all the Shaman had said. The quiet strength he exhibited as he sat across from me was like soothing balm to my wounds. I had no doubt everything would be all right now, and I would once again be well.

"Why don't I give Mom a call to come up now?" he suggested. "Are you ready, or do you need more time?"

"I don't need more time. I am ready. Thank you."

The Shaman's mother entered quietly and sat down, off to one side, adding the power of her presence through wisdom and witness to the ceremony. The lights were lowered and, from somewhere in the background, soft flute music was wafting around and through us.

The Shaman, using a feather fan, carefully wafted the smoke from a bit of white sage over himself, his Mother, and then me. He then began praying aloud in a strong, steady voice, asking The Old Ones for the right medicine to use in this particular healing. Carefully, through meditation and prayer, The Shaman put me 'in the right position,' the level of acceptance required to receive the healing. I later learned that The Old Ones require anyone asking for a healing to formally make a request, often more than once, until they feel the person is truly ready to receive the healing. It is customary for the person receiving the healing to bring a small gift to honor the Old Ones, as well as to thank them for the healing.

The ceremony that followed was powerful beyond imagining. As the Shaman had already told me, with Creator's permission, a healing circle was formed. He called each grandfather and grandmother by name as they entered the circle. When all was ready, he asked for a purging, to rid my body of all negative thoughts, feelings, and energies. When this was done, he asked me to rest for a moment. He then spread a healing blanket on the floor and assisted me in moving from my chair to the floor.

As I lay on my back, the Shaman wrapped the healing blanket entirely around me and placed a small pillow under my head. My eyes were closed; I was drifting in another time, another place. I could feel the pull of an irresistible smile tugging at my mouth. There was nothing I could do about it—nor did I want to do anything about it. I felt completely suffused with happiness, a single infinitesimal mote adrift in the universal all.

I heard the Shaman's voice from afar, asking me to call upon my totem animals to assist in my healing. Many came, and I was glad to see them. Each one who appeared brought more healing balm to put into the clean, new space that been left within me from the purging. I joyfully welcomed these, my totem animals, and as I greeted each of them, they leaped into my body, my spirit, my being, to become one with me. When guardian fox appeared, we touched noses in recognition, greeting one another with joy and understanding. When he leaped into my physical self, his beautiful big, bushy tail did not immediately fit through the opening and he had to work to pull his tail through. As from a great distance, I heard someone laughing aloud. "Who is laughing?" I wondered. And all at once I realized I was the one laughing; this caused me to laugh even more.

When, at last, my body was filled with the healing energy, and prayers were said to seal the energy within to continue working, the Shaman gave thanks to our Creator and The Old Ones for being allowed to serve as the hollow bones in the healing, and for the healing itself. Then, the Shaman began slowly and gently to return me to this time, this place.

At last, my eyes fluttered open and I beheld not the Shaman, but a huge mastodon, kneeling majestically beside me, his great trunk draped protectively over the cocoon of the healing blanket under which I rested. To each side of his trunk were great curling tusks. The sight of this huge creature sitting quietly beside me did not at all appear out of the ordinary to me. From the seclusion of my half-opened eyelashes, I watched him for long moments in a covert way and, all the while, I was aware that he not only was aware, but approved of my watching him.

"How are you feeling?" he asked. And in that moment, he was suddenly a huge bear, resting on his knees, kindly overseeing my care.

"I feel hot. I feel relaxed, absolutely wonderful. I feel better than I have felt in a long time," I replied. "I can never thank The Old Ones and you enough for the healing." Idly, I watched as he shifted from bear to mastodon, and back to bear again. He appeared to 'shimmer' back and forth quickly and with ease.

I could no longer restrain myself. I asked, "Do you know you're doing that?"

"What? Oh, you mean the shape shifting. It just happens sometimes. I don't actually feel it happening. I just look down and see a furry paw, or become aware of my trunk or tusks. It only happens when I'm totally relaxed, completely at ease, in a 'safe' environment."

"So you can't do it any time you want?" I persisted.

"We'll talk about this another time. Right now, we need to bring you 'out of it.' Let me help you sit up. Don't make any sudden moves for a while. You may feel light-headed or dizzy. I'll get you a drink of water."

Before long, I found myself driving home to the best night's rest I had enjoyed in months. When I woke up the next morning, I was totally energized. I felt wonderful. I knew, without a doubt, that there would be no more internal bleeding. That was more than ten years ago—and there has been no internal bleeding since that time.

Separation Anxiety

The days following the healing were more than chaotic. They were intense. They were unrelenting. They were eye opening. They were beyond imagining. All sorts of ancient memories began to surface. The teachings of my grandmother, which I had forgotten for so many years, resurfaced. I 'remembered' the shape shifting. I 'remembered' times gone by when each of us was connected to the Mother, our Earth, and to all the animals, and all the plants, and to the stars from whence we came. It was as if my very DNA had been reborn—reborn to the past, reborn to the person I had been waiting to become again, after so many years of my life had already elapsed. I felt I had come full circle, come home to my true self once more.

The gaining of this new self was not without discomfort, however. Intrinsically, I knew I had been healed and that the bleeding would never come again. There appeared to be great changes in me physically, as well as mentally. Overnight, my senses became so acute that it was often physically painful to hear and see. My eyesight improved to the point where ordinary daylight was a torment. Images were more than clear; they were so sharply defined that they 'hurt my eyes.'

'Ordinary' sound assailed my senses as though it were a great cacophony of unbearable proportions. More than ever before, I began to seek quiet places, quiet times.

As a child, I was always in motion, usually at the highest rate of speed I could muster, whether it was running, walking, mowing the lawn 'by hand,' shoveling snow, engaging in sports, or just playing games with friends. My parents often expressed the opinion that I was 'high-strung.' I had emerged from my hypersensitive, emotionally fragile childhood remarkably intact; in fact, I had become a confident, out-going, and mentally tough person, unhampered by negative 'baggage.'

Following the healing, I was quick to realize I was on overload—even for me. I needed help, and I needed it fast! The day after the healing, I telephoned the Shaman to ask for help. "You were right to call me," he said. "Come over after work."

After a hard day at work, coupled with constantly being bombarded with intense light and sound, I was agitated when I arrived at the Shaman's home. "I don't know what's going on," I said. "Something is wrong. Everything is so intense. And there's a feeling of loss." I started to cry.

"Not to worry," he said. "Take a chair. What you're experiencing happens sometimes. It's fairly 'normal.' When you have sustained a draining illness of long duration, such as you just went through, you're not necessarily aware of how weak you have become. Then, when healing has occurred, you feel so much better —in comparison, it is sometimes physically painful just to see and hear. The Old Ones can adjust your energy level to a lower vibration and you will feel better in no time."

"What about this feeling of loss? What is that?"

"The feelings you are experiencing are nothing more than separation anxiety. Through your healing, collective memories are beginning to flood back into your consciousness. You are remembering our Creator's gift to us, the ancient knowledge of our DNA imprinting, which 'civilization' has systematically and almost unobtrusively programmed out of most of us. Our Creator and The Old Ones, because you remember them, will now, again, be a part of you and you will forever be a part of them. Having felt their loving presence, you now miss their touch. It's as though a part of you, yourself, have gone missing."

"What do I do, just learn to live with the pain of these intense sensations?"

The Shaman laughed. "No! That is not an option. You need to remember that pain is vastly overrated. Find ways to celebrate your life, on all occasions! Don't just endure your life; it is a gift. Never give power to the negative forces you may encounter. Remember,

125

our Creator is always just a prayer away. And you may call upon the Old Ones to ask for their advice or help any time."

Sitting directly across from me, the Shaman took my hands and began to pray. He asked for a lessening of the vibration frequency of my personal energy. The prayer was very long. I began to feel as though my hands had 'gone to sleep' when I made a startling discovery. For the first of many, many times over the course of the next several years, during prayers or meditations done together, such a state of complete being existed between the Shaman and me that it was impossible to tell where one hand began and the other ended. Our energy was so in synch that neither of us could tell where the skin of one person ended and the skin of the other began.

When he finished the prayer, we sat together quietly still holding hands. Neither of us spoke; each of us was aware of the uniqueness of our situation.

Reluctantly, we at last let go of one another's hands. The Shaman looked deeply into my eyes. It seemed to me he was looking into my very soul. "Go now, and grieve no more," he said. "The time for mourning is at an end. Now is a time for living. Now is the time for new beginnings."

The Thousand-Mile Think

The following week, I placed the beautiful wooden box containing my husband's ashes on the front passenger seat of the car, securing it in place with towels. I checked the house one last time and put my suitcases in the trunk of the car. Tippy and I were soon 'on the road again' driving North to Illinois.

Years before, Howard had 'fallen in love' with the old-fashioned cemetery where my folks were to be buried. He liked the natural landscaping of the graceful old trees and the flowers that were planted in the ground in front of the headstones. Howard liked this cemetery so much that he talked my folks into selling him the extra plots they had secured, so that he and I would eventually lie next to Mom and Dad.

Tippy was a seasoned traveler; he had spent a major portion of his life traveling by land, sea, and air. When traveling by car or motor home, he liked to watch the scenery, and especially liked to see big animals like cows or horses. He often put his head out the open window, depending on how fast we were driving. I enjoy driving, and the trip was relaxing. It was fun to be going somewhere once again, not knowing what challenges lay around the next bend in the road. I simply trusted to chance that all would be well. I liked to say, not entirely in jest, "What I like best is going to the edge of the world, and then just throwing myself off the edge." Fortunately, Howard was not only of the same ilk, but even more so than I. We were very lucky to enjoy a lot of great adventures together.

Even when my husband was living and we made this trip together, I always referred to it, jokingly, as 'the thousand mile think.' I spent hours going over every aspect of my life. I continually 'reinvented myself,' as it were. In actuality, I conducted a mini-life review, so I could evaluate and make changes I considered 'for the better.'

Besides Tippy and I 'being on our own,' I soon became aware that this trip was shaping up to be not just different from past trips, but much 'more than special.' Driving for hours on the open road is often mesmerizing and I was slow to realize that Tippy and I were not alone; in fact, our small car was quite crowded. A host of Native American Grandmothers had joined us. They laughed and talked pleasantly among themselves at length. I did not understand their language at first, but that was quickly remedied. All at once, I realized I was able to read their thoughts, and they mine.

"You remember us now, don't you, daughter?"

I was dumbfounded, mulling the question over, and did not immediately answer.

"When you were so sick with the high fever?" one of them prompted.

"That was you?" I asked. "I was so irritated. I could hear your voices, but you must have been just 'out of range,' and I couldn't hear what was being said. I was aware that topics of importance were being discussed, and I felt so left out. I was really angry that I couldn't hear you."

"You weren't supposed to hear what was said at that time. You were a child, and not yet prepared enough to understand. You had a really high fever—105.8 degrees Fahrenheit, for over twenty-four straight hours. We had our hands full just keeping your brain from being damaged. But we did want you to know that we were there to help you, and to reassure you that everything would be okay."

I thought back to that time of childhood sickness, so long ago. I remember hearing the Grandmothers murmuring, but before long, my anger abated, and I drifted into a very deep sleep.

The following morning, when I awakened, the sunlight filtering through the crumbled plaster and broken lathe slats of my bedroom walls onto my coverlet was so bright that it hurt my eyes. Gradually, my eyes became accustomed to the sun's intensity, and I became entranced by the dancing patterns of light flitting merrily about the room.

My joy was increased when I realized I could breathe through both nostrils once more. Greedily, I inhaled deep gulps of crisp, sweet air into my lungs. The air was so cold, my nostrils hurt. Tears sprang to my eyes.

My mother entered, carrying a tray. "Good morning," she said. "I thought maybe you might feel like eating a little something."

I looked at the shallow soup bowl she offered and began to salivate. Two large slices of homemade white bread had been lightly toasted, slathered in butter, and stacked butter side up on the bottom of the bowl. Barely enough warm milk had been poured over all to saturate the toast, leaving just a bit of butter-flecked milk floating around the toast. The whole of this had been lightly salted. Quite possibly, this was the best food I ever ate. I certainly thought so at the time.

I felt much better after eating. No sooner had I finished eating my breakfast than I fell into a light, refreshing sleep. When I awakened several hours later, I was ravenous.

At lunchtime, the hamburger arrived. This was a big event, as meat was often in short supply in our home. As children, we always knew when we were on the upswing from illness because the hamburger would arrive, pressed firmly between two slices of bread with a little catsup on each side, and neatly sliced on the diagonal. This was our signal that the time of illness was easing and we would soon be strong and well again.

I smiled at these childhood memories as I returned to the present. "Why are you here now, Grandmothers?"

"We need your help. The Shaman is ill."

"The Shaman is ill?" I stupidly repeated. How could that be? "I'm really sorry to hear that, but what could I possibly do to help? I'm not a healer."

"Oh, but you are." The sound of their laughter was musical.

"I wouldn't know how to begin, or what to do," I protested.

"No one does in the beginning. It's not a matter of learning; it's a matter of simply remembering what to do. Your knowledge is already complete. It simply needs to be re-awakened."

"Will the Shaman allow me to help?"

"Yes, of course. He has been waiting for you."

Mile after mile rolled by, as the Grandmothers helped me to remember the ancient ways, the arts of healing, and I felt the irrefutable ring of truth in all of their words.

"First of all, never refer to yourself as I, or me. The acceptance of the Good Red Road, your true path, begins with giving up the ego. The proper way of showing honor and respect when praying to Creator, or addressing The Old Ones, is to refer to self as 'This One.'"

"There are many ways of healing. Some heal with plants. Some pray. Some do ceremonies. Some dance. Some have so much love to give that love alone heals. Some even follow the White Man's medicine. Sometimes it is a combination of one or more of these medicines. The Shaman serves as a Hollow Bones for the Grandfathers and us. You, too, will serve as a Hollow Bones. As such, you must remember this—all of us serve as representatives of our Great Creator, Wakan Tanka Tunka Silla, no matter what form the healing takes. The great strength of the healing energy, the power evidenced by healing is not ours to claim; everything emanates from our Creator."

"There is no wrong way to heal, if that healing comes from the purity of the heart and by the Grace of our Creator. It is important to remember that healing and curing are not always the same. Many who are healed appear to be no better physically and, in fact, may suffer further failing health and may ultimately cross, as a result of their illness. This can be devastating to the healer. He or she may feel they have not done a good job of healing. When acting as a Hollow Bones, it is essential that you not think with your linear mind. Remember that the agreement between the person and Creator was decided before the person was born into this time. Remember—the person has indeed been healed! The person has been healed in the way that was most needed for him or her."

"Some of our healing methods are the same, or similar, but usually each of us will have one particular medicine that is thought to be his or her specialty. Our Creator has given us many gifts, many healing tools, many avenues of hope. Any or all of these great gifts may be used alone, severally, or in conjunction, one with the other. No medicine lessens the power of any other medicine. It is akin to lighting a brand from the fire—it does not lessen the power or spirit of the fire, yet the brand exists as a brightly lit separate entity on its own. So it is when more than one medicine is needed."

"How will I know what medicine to use?" I asked.

"Every case is unique, and will require asking the Grandfathers and us, the Grandmothers, for our advice on the subject. As we mentioned before, you, too, are a Hollow Bones. We will begin by showing you how to heal the Shaman. His healing won't happen overnight. He is very tired. He is worn out. Your job will be to heal his body, his mind, and his spirit. In return, he will heal your body, your mind, and your spirit. Together, you will work to heal others. He will be your teacher; you will learn from him, in just the same ways, as healing knowledge was shared and passed on from one to another in generations past. You will feel the strength and honor of this union with so many, many medicine people, holy people, who have served before you.

"The Shaman and you will be a powerful symbiotic unit. You will learn to love one another in every way; this love will be as natural as breathing. You will mistakenly think you will be together forever. But that is not to be the case. When you have learned your lessons from one another, you need to go forward to further learning. You will forget that we have told you this until it happens, and deny it when it comes. Everything will seem to negate the idea of parting. This parting will be very painful for each of you, but we will be there to help you, and a new way will be found for each of you to continue to be stronger, and more able healers. You will embark on separate journeys, secure in the truth of the rightness of knowing one another, but continuing on your journeys towards new growth, to new teachers, to new knowledge. Each of you has grown through love of one another. You will never be separated in spirit. You, daughter, will be like the brand that was lit from the fire. You will be as a bright, independent entity, able to light other fires, but having taken nothing away from the main fire of the Shaman."

"I have a thousand questions," I said.

"Now is not the time for questions. Now is a time for honoring your husband, to complete the circle you and your husband shared. Go now, daughter, remember your husband, and the wonderful life you shared together. Revel in the closeness you enjoyed for so long. We will be here for you."

Coming Home

Home, sweet home!

I have enjoyed three marriages. To friends who ask if I will marry again I always say, "No, I don't think so. I have bagged my limit. Let's give somebody else a chance." Throughout each of those marriages, a total of twenty-eight years, I had always worked to establish a comfortable, loving home for my husband and family, a home where visitors and extended family alike would feel welcome and at ease. I must confess that I am a 'died-in-the-wool homebody.' I truly enjoy being 'at home' with my dog. It is just the two of us now. We spend time taking long walks and enjoying 'playtime' together. Often, I spend time just puttering around, not doing much at all, except relaxing. I love reading and generally have several books 'going' at once. Often, I relax into a quiet meditation with my companion at my side. Life is good.

In spite of establishing, and in some cases building, numerous homes over the years, there was really only one home—and that home was wherever my mother lived. As it happened, she was still living in the home she and Dad had bought more than forty years before. Our family moved to this home when I began high school. Mom and Dad had lived there together until Dad's death in 1983. Fortunately, Mother's health was such that she was able to maintain and enjoy living in the family home until a month before her death.

Whenever any of us returned home, it was as though we had never left. There was always such an air of excitement and expectation to our homecomings. Mother was always there to greet us with open arms, plenty of good food, and the inevitable cup of strong, hot coffee. The coffee pot was always 'on' at Mother's, and friends and relatives would come and go at all hours. Impromptu gatherings made Mom's home an ongoing 'open house.' She loved the company, and everyone who visited felt singled out for special welcome.

My husband, Howard, loved to 'come home' to Mom's. He always said it reminded him of his parents' home when he was growing up. And Mom spoiled him outrageously. He loved it. He soaked up her attention like a sponge.

Mom loved to cook, loved to throw parties; we teased her, calling her 'the hostess with the most-est,' and I think she was secretly pleased with this title. My husband absolutely loved good food and he was in his glory at Mother's, enjoying second and third helpings. She was in her glory, as well. Our father had been a 'picky eater.' He rarely enjoyed food the way the rest of us did, and mostly made a show of eating until it was time to give his food to the cats. So it was a great joy for my mother to see how much my Howard enjoyed her food. He and Mom were fast friends.

Refreshed by fond memories, I found myself once again resuming my journey.

The Spiritual Marriage

As the Grandmothers had taught me, I began to serve as a healer to the Shaman. He, in turn became my healer, my teacher, and my friend. Inevitably, our relationship became so close that it transcended friendship. We came to love one another. We had known from our first meeting that our time together would be limited, that we were not intended to become life partners, but would always remain spiritually connected far beyond any physical sense.

Whenever the Shaman and I were together, the Grandfathers and Grandmothers would gather around us, enfolding us in the safe, loving cocoon of their great wisdom, guiding and protecting us as they helped us to new understanding.

Always aware that our spiritual path transcended time and space, we were only a little surprised as memories of past lives enjoyed together, began to surface. The spiritual marriage described here, occurred not only in this lifetime but with variations in other tandem lifetimes, as well. Because all time is all time, these physical unions were exponential in bringing about an even greater spiritual union, a more powerful healing union, a truly expanded awareness.

And so we relived, and lived anew, our togetherness. Our lodge was lit only by firelight; in the distance, we could hear the people celebrating our marriage. The drum seemed to be the very essence of our hearts beating in unison. Dancing, singing, and feasting had become the fabric of the night. The Shaman spread a large black bear skin on the lodge 'floor.' In an unhurried, smooth motion, he loosed the ties at the shoulders of my buckskin dress and eased me down to lie upon the bearskin.

I watched in fascination as he kneeled beside me and began to free his long hair from the rawhide ties that had secured his braids. He used his fingers as a 'comb.' Before long, his hair was loose, hanging below his shoulder blades, and halfway down his chest. The Shaman's hair was thick, black as a raven wing, and liberally laced with threads of silver. He was a powerful figure, strong and sure, yet sensitive and caring. I was completely entranced.

In a single fluid motion, the Shaman sat down beside me, legs crossed comfortably, and with uplifted palms resting on his knees, he began to pray out loud. His prayer was long and, as I listened to the soothing cadence of his voice, I gradually became aware that The Old Ones had begun to gather, as was their practice when the

Shaman and I were together.

When the prayers were finished, he began to sing in a pleasant, low voice. I did not understand the words, but not knowing, still I understood. The message was clear. This Ceremony from the Time Before marked the beginning of a new bonding between the Shaman and This One, a bonding that not only incorporated but also easily eclipsed all that had gone before.

I watched, as from afar, as the Shaman rose to his knees, let his long hair fall forward over his face, and, beginning with my forehead, began slowly and gently to brush my face with his hair. He continued this delightful path, moving his head from side to side, up and down, 'painting' my body with the brush of his hair, as though my body were his favorite canvas, until at last he came to the tip of my toes.

He then gently turned me onto my stomach to begin the entire brushing sequence again, this time working down my back to my toes. Again, he turned me to lie on my back. His lips touched mine in an 'electric kiss.'

Later, as I lay in his arms, he spoke softly to me, "Now we are as one."

I was later to learn that this Ceremony is very ancient, and stems from the belief that each hair on our heads is a sacred conduit to Creator, that by virtue of fusing our spiritual, mental, and physical selves, one to the other, we indeed become one, not only to one another, but one with the Great Mystery.

Collective Memory and Natural Law

Each of us has within us a collective memory; we have genetic imprinting in every single cell of our bodies. It could be said that within each of us, we possess all of the universal knowledge that ever existed. This knowledge, obviously, has a long memory. This knowledge carries back to a time when it was possible to understand everything in the surrounding world known at that time. The properties and uses of our plant relations were known. We were able not only to understand the ways of our animal friends, but also to communicate freely with them. There were more animals then, different ones who have since ceased to exist as a species.

In those days, no one needed to speak aloud. All communication took place telepathically, whether within intimate family groups, larger tribal groups, or with roving bands of hunters far away. Distances proved no obstacle to communication in those days.

Why don't we enjoy the simplicity and immediacy of such telepathic thought sharing these days? Some of us do. But for the most part, as our environment changed to accommodate 'civilization,' most people lost the ability to communicate except through verbal avenues. The gift of verbal communication was tempered, for the first time in history, by the ability to deceive, whether by accident, or design, and thus began the progression of 'modern' communication attributed to 'civilization.'

As more and more 'sophisticated' DNA imprinting took place, the old ways of understanding and communicating were pushed further and further into the recesses of collective memory. And yet today, with thousands and thousands of years of separation between us and our earliest progenitors, with the frenetic activity of the hectic modern world we live in forcing us further away from our past knowledge, still—ancient memory serves.

Each of us, no matter how modern our thinking, responds to the simplest, most elemental survival quotients:

Fight or flight stands strongly at the forefront; the struggle for survival is an ingrained imperative.

We protect our young at all costs.

We have built-in mechanisms for survival of the species—modern-day versions of submission—methods for backing down gracefully. We also provide for avenues of escape, thus allowing the other person to back down and save face.

We often implement avoidance, averting conflict before it occurs; for instance, when walking toward a stranger, avoiding eye contact with that person presents no opening for misunderstanding or unfounded aggression.

We still understand, at a base level, the importance of respecting territorial imperatives—especially as pertains to 'personal space.' Personal space varies from person to person, culture to culture. Some cultures promote people standing much closer to one another than others. Evolutionary and environmental perceptions appear to be responsible for how much space each of us requires as a personal comfort zone. Cultures where large populations thrive within small confines naturally dictate closer personal space. Those nurtured in wide-open spaces, require a significantly larger personal space than others. Each of us seeks our own comfort zone, our own 'close' zone, responding to our genetically imprinted needs.

The relentless advance of civilization has complicated our perception about the ancient programming we have inherited; for instance, in the 'close-standing' cultures, it is considered good manners and a mark of special favor to share personal space with someone. Conversely, when the 'close standing' person interacts with a more 'space requiring' individual, and seeks to honor that individual by standing close, only to see the other person continue to back away, misunderstanding and upset occurs as each person involved thinks the other to be rude and insensitive.

The above are just a few instances of ancient genetic DNA coding. The larger our worldwide population has become, the more diverse our environments and cultures, the less commonality expressed, the greater the risk for survival of humankind.

How do we avoid annihilation of most or all life on this beloved Mother, this spectacularly diverse and beautiful Turtle Island?

The answer is simple and irrefutable: we must return to an acceptance and understanding of Natural Law.

Natural Law is the wellspring from which all order flows.

Natural Law is the single, underlying, remaining common denominator for all life of every conceivable kind.

Natural Law is not negotiable or open to change or argument. Natural Law is intrinsic, unmovable, unchanging, beyond question. Natural Law simply IS.

The Perfect Leaf

Mother and I always had a difficult relationship. It was complicated, and I doubt either of us truly understood the depth of it. On the surface, we were as night and day. If one of us expressed approval for a particular subject, the other automatically took the part of 'Naysayer.'

Mother, as a sensitive child, had endured the multitude of terrible indignities engendered by the poverty visited upon her family. She and her own Mother did not communicate well, and were often at odds. Grandmother, to all accounts, was emotionally remote from my mother. And yet, they truly loved one another and supported one another 'through thick and thin.'

Obviously, my relationship with my mother was nothing more than 'history repeating itself.' I was the firstborn, and the only child in our family singled out for this special legacy. Both my siblings agree that I was the only one who received this treatment.

I was a difficult child. In order to survive the world of alcoholism, insensitivity, and debilitating poverty, which was my lot, I developed tremendous mental toughness. My body was not quite so adept at surviving; I suffered from anemia, allergies, and asthma attacks that were so severe that I would be in bed, gasping for breath, for as much as three days at a time.

In between bouts of asthma, I tested my mother's patience to the limits, and often paid the price for my recklessness. Out of her own frustration and helplessness, Mom would often lash out, hitting me so hard and at such length that it stopped just short of being described as beating. She would hit me as hard as she could until she was so worn out that she was gasping for breath. On one occasion, she hit me with such force that she broke one of the big veins in her hand. Throughout these episodes, I stubbornly refused to cry—in front of anyone. I cried plenty when I was alone, however. When Mom broke the vein in her hand, I could tell it hurt her a lot. Being the obstinate child I was, I looked up at her and said, "Is that all you got?" I braced myself for a new onslaught of blows, but surprisingly, none came. "Go to your room," my Mother sobbed. For once in my lifetime, I did as I was told, and in that instant, I felt very ashamed of myself and vowed to 'be a better daughter.' None of the spankings were ever that bad again. It was as though each of us had reached some sort of unspoken, tacit agreement. We had come full circle and arrived back at ground zero—a neutral zone for each of us, where we learned to respect one another's boundaries and, thereafter, stopped just short of said boundaries.

I always felt my mother disapproved of me on all occasions, and yet, when I needed help or support, she was always there for me—and vice versa. We were engaged the whole of our lives in a strange symbiotic dance. The one thing I know for sure about this beleaguered, complex woman is that in spite of feeling that Mother truly did not like or approve of my actions, she always loved me. And I loved her. I loved Mother more than I can say, or even think about. She was such a part of me. I always missed her, wherever I was, whatever I was doing. Also, I liked and admired her. She accomplished a lot in her life against heavy odds. Eventually, we came to a comfortable place to be—together.

A mark of Mother's love for me that was tangible, which I fondly remember each new autumn, is that each year, no matter where I was, or how old I was, or what my circumstances, she always sent me a perfect leaf. This leaf came, through the postal service, without warning or explanation. It was usually a maple leaf, pressed gently between paper towels and cardboard, in the full glory of changing colors—green, gold, red, and coral—an ongoing affirmation of eternal life and eternal love. What a great gift! And she knew I would understand and treasure her gift. She used to say that actions speak louder than words.

Each new autumn since Mother's death six years ago, as I walk with my dear companion dog and the colored leaves fall on us like rain, I am reminded of my mother's great gifts to me. And I feel her presence and her love, stronger than ever, as we go forward in new understanding of one another.

149

So once again, life comes full circle, with each new circle continuing to enhance and enrich our spiritual paths, our spiritual center, teaching us harmony.

Thank you for the perfect leaves, Mother. I love you, too.

A Holy Place

We were on our way! We had been driving for hours, first on blacktop roads, then gravel, and for some time now, a series of one dirt road after another. The road we were presently traveling had narrowed to become a single lane. In this vast deserted area, there appeared to be little chance of encountering another vehicle, so we fairly flew over the road with relative impunity, leaving a huge dust contrail behind us.

"What's the hurry?" I asked as we fishtailed around a particularly tight curve in the road.

"You'll see." The Shaman laughed.

Minutes passed when, reflectively, the Shaman intoned,

"There is a time for going in, and there is a time for coming out. These times must be respected and honored beyond understanding; they must never be violated."

"What if something happens that you can't get back out 'in time'?" I asked.

"Serious consequences are attached," the Shaman sidestepped. "All we need to know is that we are honored guests here, and as such, must not overstay our welcome."

The dusty road abruptly ended, spreading out into a relatively flat, level area surrounded by huge boulders. Gravel and rocks of all sizes comprised the surface we stepped onto as we got out of the truck.

I turned slowly in a full circle, breathing in the amazing landscape that surrounded us. Nearby boulders appeared to be as big as houses and cars. Some sat alone, like majestic sentinels, on guard. Others nestled together in great stacks, like sleeping puppies.

I felt light-headed. I was acutely aware of the oven-hot heat emanating from these huge rocks. I felt I might be sick to my stomach. I could feel not a breath of air stirring. I found myself in a suddenly surreal world, as alien as though I had just landed on the moon. I felt extremely dizzy and there was a buzzing noise in my ears. It was all I could do to keep from fainting. Slowly, I became aware of the soothing music of tiny wings, rising and falling in rhythmic motion, which abruptly came to a halt. I looked down to see a small honeybee sitting on my hand, looking up at me in an alert, calming way. I smiled. My new friend smiled back at me. Magically, I suddenly felt fine; I felt more than fine. My newfound euphoric state found me gently floating above the ground.

I glanced at the Shaman to see if he noticed that I was floating off the ground. He chuckled softly in acknowledgement of my newfound state of freedom. "The rock people are very shy, so they have asked their friend, the honeybee, to 'speak' for them. You have officially been welcomed by the rock people.

"You must be very special for the rock people to have shared their energy with you upon first meeting," the Shaman continued. He grinned in an engaging way. "Wait a minute," he continued. "They say that they have gladly shared their energy with you because you will need their added strength to enjoy, and learn from, our journey today.

"Are you ready?" he asked.

"Ready!" was my eager response.

Quickly, the Shaman removed a large leather bag from the truck, along with a large canteen of water. As he slung these over his shoulder, he advised me, "Follow closely in my footsteps. Each time you take a step, make sure your foot is placed exactly within my footprint. This is very important." As an afterthought, he added, "I'll take shorter steps so you won't have a problem." At six feet, six inches tall, and weighing three hundred well-muscled pounds, the Shaman presented as an impressive figure. Naturally, his stride would far outpace my five and a half foot stretch, long legs and all.

And so we began this day's journey. What began as a barren, rock-strewn landscape quickly gave way to a very dense, brushy area. Our way proved to be slow going, because of the numerous brambles and berry bushes that continually scratched us and snagged our clothes. It almost seemed as if the bushes, the brush itself, attempted to deny us passage.

It was terrifically hot without a breath of air moving. I began to sweat profusely and felt winded. "May we stop and rest for a bit?" I asked.

"No, I'm sorry. We need to keep moving." The Shaman offered me the canteen. "Take a sip of water. Don't just drink it down or you'll get cramps. Hold it in your mouth for a little, gently swishing it around, and then slowly swallow it." He reached down and picked up a smooth, fairly flat rock about the size of an elongated quarter, quickly rubbing the sand and dirt from it. "Put this in your mouth—and don't swallow it," he laughed. "That's an old Indian trick," he added. "We've been doing this for centuries."

A few sips of tepid water, coupled with holding a rock in my mouth, had given me new perspective. It was impossible not to think about the rock and the significance of that rock, held, so tentatively at first, in my mouth. The rock was beautiful—dark, smooth, oval in shape, highlighted by a lighter-colored vein of a different rock composition, which feathered out in a unique design. I no longer felt thirsty, and I was no longer tired. In fact, I felt quite good, anticipating the adventure that lay ahead. I felt quietly energized.

Our brushy 'path' led us downhill, the brush becoming less prevalent as we traveled. A cool breeze began to gently caress my hot face. "What is that noise?" I thought to myself. I struggled to identify the special music I was hearing. And suddenly, there it was —a rushing stream, shining silver in the reflected sunlight, hurrying to a distant place, an ongoing ribbon of frothing water, bracketed by lush green grass, reeds, flowers, and trees.

I was so excited that I fairly shouted to the Shaman, "Just look!"

"Shush," he admonished, holding a finger to his lips. "We need to be very quiet."

"Why?" I whispered.

"This place is home to some of the Little People. Above all else they value peace and quiet, and they don't much care for 'outsiders.' If we're quiet, we may catch a glimpse of them. Sometimes you can hear them talking or laughing among themselves. They can be very mischievous sometimes. But they are very wise, and their Nation is very old. They have been 'around' for a long time."

"What do we do if we see them?" I wanted to know.

"We respect their privacy. We don't try to speak to them, and above all, don't stare. And absolutely, under no circumstances, try to touch them.

"Remember that we are here at their sufferance. The continuation of our journey will only be possible with their approval and permission. Without that permission, we can go no further. These Little People are Gate Keepers."

"Gate Keepers," I breathed. "Gate Keepers," I thought aloud. "This is definitely food for thought."

I concentrated, afraid of losing my footing on the slippery stones in the stream. I stepped carefully from stone to stone, following in the Shaman's footsteps—exactly as he had instructed. We continued on in silence, the meandering pattern of the stones slowly stretching out in a lengthy diagonal across the stream.

I breathed a sigh of relief as we stepped onto the far shore, having avoided disturbing the Gate Keepers by unceremoniously falling into the stream, and thus disquieting their home place. So far, so good—the Shaman nodded approvingly at me as we continued walking.

Later, on the drive home, the Shaman regaled me with a story told to him by a friend who had been drawn to this area. The person was at a bad time in his life and openly admitted denying the old ways; he had come inebriated and in a combative mood to this sacred place. He had openly and loudly disrespected the Little People by being boisterous and obnoxious, refusing to honor the times of going in and the times of coming out. The arrogance of this person in denying this ancient dictate was repaid by his being thrown down into the stream, not once, but several times. As he related the tale to the Shaman, he said it was like suddenly running into a brick wall, being hurled into the stream and held down until

156

he could no longer breathe. He thought he was going to drown for sure, and blacked out.

He came back to consciousness some time later, laid out on the bank of the stream with the sound of the rushing water coursing through his body. The sun was shining through the leaves of a tree, dancing in dappling, mischievous, lazy dots over his face. A cool breeze seemed to be cleansing his spirit. Thinking he had died and gone to a better place, the young man opened his eyes—and beheld standing all around him smiling Little People. He remembered hearing the sound of many, tiny, tinkling bells, each ringing in a different tonal range. "He will be alright now," the bells rang out.

The young man slept, and when he awakened, he related to the Shaman that it was as if he were reborn. He was no longer angry. He felt centered and energized. He had a dream, he said, where the ancestors had come to him, taken him to ceremony, and given back to him the proud heritage that was his by blood.

That day, the young man who was drawn by an impulse he didn't understand to this holy place continued his journey on the Good Red Road with new understanding, new insight, and a newfound dedication to understanding and embracing the powerful mysteries and knowledge of The Old Ones.

The Shaman and I now climbed steadily upward, the terrain becoming more difficult by the minute as we tried to find firm footing among the sandy, heavily rock-strewn debris under our feet. Not far ahead of us stood a towering pyramid of rocks. The Shaman indicated by a nod of his head that this, indeed, was our destination. My heart sank as I briefly surveyed this seemingly insurmountable obstacle.

As if reading my mind, the Shaman turned and briefly encircled my shoulders, giving me a quick hug of encouragement, and said, "Take my hand." And so, in this way, we climbed steadily upward, lost in thought, lost in time.

All at once, we were at the top of the pyramid. In wonder, we looked out over the vast panoramic view spread before us. The multitudes of huge rocks arrayed below seemed small and far away.

It seemed to me that we were at the very pinnacle of the world; certainly, we felt very close to the sun. I imagined that I could actually see the heat waves radiating back from the huge rocks of the pyramid on which we now stood.

"Come this way," the Shaman intoned softly. Before us lay a fairly flat rock, centered at the very top of the pyramid. "Please," he continued, "sit down; be comfortable."

We seated ourselves in a cross-legged easy way. "Before we begin our prayers, we need to take a sip of water," the Shaman advised, offering me the canteen. Carefully, I removed the rock from my mouth and slipped it into a pocket. Tentatively, I took a few sips of the tepid water, holding it in my mouth briefly before swallowing. The absence of the 'moisture-holding' rock in my mouth seemed to leave a big space, and I kept exploring the inside of my closed mouth with my tongue. It felt as if a major part of me were missing. I found myself thinking about all of this at length, running through my mind what the significance of this observation might be.

My meditative state was put on hold when the Shaman said, "Let's begin."

The Shaman began by purifying each of us with the fragrant smoke of burning white sage. He then set the sage aside to finish burning in the seashell he had brought with us. He then offered gifts of tobacco to the four directions.

Then, seated at the 'top of the world,' sitting cross-legged across from one another, the Shaman began to sing a prayer song. He then offered prayers aloud, as did I, before relaxing into a joint meditation.

My eyes were closed and I relaxed into the rock I was seated on. I felt the very faint breeze brushing my face, hot from the kiss of the sun. I breathed in faint unidentifiable aromas from the surrounding area, as well as the scent of the burning sage mingled with the mildly astringent salty scents of our clean perspirations.

The fierce wind seemed to spin out in endless, invisible gossamer strands, lost against the unbroken expanse of the blue-white sky. Faint voices came to me on the wind, which seemed to escalate until they were completely audible. With surprise, I realized I was able to understand the language they were speaking.

I looked down from the pyramid to see all kinds of activity taking place. A large village was spread out before us, a virtual 'beehive of activity.' Everywhere, people were busily engaged in working and playing. And the desert was no longer there. Instead, a green landscape abounded. Carefully tilled fields were richly populated with growing crops. Corn and squash were being cultivated, as well as a few rows of wild onions.

Not far from the village, we noticed large patches of wild berries being picked by clutches of laughing girls who appeared to eat as many berries as they picked. They were in high spirits, running from bush to bush, quickly stripping the berries and dropping them into straw baskets they carried.

Hides were being stretched and scraped.

Food was being prepared and cooked over open fires.

Women gathered to sew and gossip, seated in shady areas.

Grandmothers carefully watched over younger children, instructing them from time to time, in various ways.

Grandfathers were painstakingly helping the young ones to learn the skills necessary to sustain physical life—bow and arrow making, flint knapping, knife making, how to stalk and hunt.

Just beyond the village, a Medicine Man quietly directed a group of youngsters to 'spread out' in search of medicinal plants. He had shown them how to carefully gather the plants he was in need of at this time.

To my surprise, I realized there was a storyteller present. My surprise stemmed from the knowledge that story telling was usually a cold-weather activity, and clearly, it was Summer time.

160

The Storyteller moved easily from one working group to the next, staying no longer than three or four fingers measured against the sun. He worked his craft, his listeners spellbound, not just by the 'entertainment' being presented, but by a sense of the rich history and traditions of the People that they effortlessly absorbed. Each story was a venue for value lessons on integrity, protocol, respect, honor, and truth.

Not everyone was present in the village this day. Parties were out hunting. Some were away trading. A few had gone to visit relatives in another village. Fewer still were away on personal 'business,' not the least of which was vision questing.

Atop our lofty perch, the Shaman and I found ourselves totally entranced by the joyous laughter of children at play. Looking back, I still hear those laughing children, and it never fails to bring a smile to my face.

Over the years, I have had many thoughts about what the Shaman and I witnessed that day. I have considered that we somehow 'went back in time.'

I also considered that perhaps what we saw that day was simply a triggered response, drawn from our collective memory, and that we were simply 'seeing' the village from this standpoint.

The idea that really resonated, however, was one of my grandmother's first teachings, "All time is all time." This thought kept coming back to me, causing me to consider that today, 'this time,' and yesterday, 'the time before,' even tomorrow, are occurring simultaneously 'in the now.'

Because we cannot readily see the village today, does it mean the village isn't still there? Or that it is a figment of imagination? Or that it never existed at all? I think not. I truly believe the village is as 'alive and well' today as ever.

If you listen carefully—ever so carefully—you may hear the laughter of children!

The Way of The Red Hand

As my Native American journey continued, my ancestry seemed to refocus at my very center, calling forth elusive bits and pieces of a distant, forgotten, collective memory. And, as my consciousness continued to expand, many symbols began to appear to me in dreams and visions. So it was with The Red Hand.

Grandfather Ka-tah-na-shea was the first to bring the Red Hand to my attention. It happened in the following way:

On a given day, as so often happened, the Shaman and I were in a joint meditation. With Great Creator's permission, we had asked that the Grandfathers and Grandmothers be allowed to convene a healing circle for a friend, who lived far away. Though it seemed like mere moments, we had been 'under' for some time. At the conclusion of the successful ceremony, as always, we gave thanks to the Grandfathers and Grandmothers for their healing ministrations, and then to Wakan Tanka Tunka Silla for sanctioning the ceremony.

The Shaman's voice came to me from a great distance as he encouraged me gently to return to 'reality.' The return was always difficult for me, but I was making an effort to 'swim to the surface' when my attention was so abruptly snapped back to the spirit world that it was like an electric shock. I heard myself gasp for breath.

"Wait," I managed to say. "Someone wishes to speak."

I felt the Shaman, seated directly in front of me, take my hands in his. "What do you see?" he asked.

"There is a man. He is lying down—on a rock, I think. The rock is about the size of a twin bed. It is raised off the ground, about waist high. Just as you were calling me from the meditation, a Grandfather raised himself up on one elbow and reached a hand toward me to call me back. It was a great effort for him. He is very weak."

"What does he look like?" the Shaman asked.

"Well, for one thing, he has a very dignified appearance. He is well made and very statesman-like; he seems to be a man to be reckoned with. He appears to be in his fifties. It's hard to tell because he is lying down, but he appears to be tall and moderate of build—not especially muscular, but very strong. You can feel his

164

strength, even as weak as he is."

"What else?" the Shaman urged.

"Well, there is something I don't understand at all," I replied. "Everything is blue. Even the man is blue. The man's clothing is blue. The man's skin is blue. The rock he lies upon is blue, and around the man, all things are blue. The shadows and recesses in his clothes and the surroundings are a slightly darker blue, but still blue." I paused for breath, before continuing, "What does this mean?"

"Blue is the color of the Spirit World," the Shaman explained. "This man is in the Spirit World. I will speak with him."

"Grandfather, do you see me?" he asked.

"I see you, Nephew. I am glad to see you."

"How may we help you, Grandfather?"

"I have a message for the People. I have been here for a long time now, but I can see that things are not going well for the young ones in present times."

The Grandfather paused for breath for a few minutes. To the Shaman and me, it seemed an eternity. We waited anxiously to see if he would continue. Finally, with a great effort, the Grandfather began, once more, to speak.

"The People have forgotten the old ways. They have lost their center. They honor the ego now, and the ego is always hungry. They struggle to feed the ego, but it is never enough. This is confusing and disheartening to the People. They have become fearful, and their fear causes them to behave foolishly. They abuse their bodies with strong drink and practice vulgarity. They no longer behave with honor towards themselves or their elders. They have ceased to practice good values, but instead continue to harm themselves and one another. I hear the People crying. They are crying out to me to find a way to become whole again, to live in health and harmony. That is why I have called to you, Nephew, and to you, Daughter. Will you help me?"

"It will be our great honor, Grandfather," the Shaman replied. "We are happy to be so chosen."

"I must rest now," the Grandfather sighed as he lay down once more. "We will meet often and find a way to help the people."

Slowly, the Grandfather, his 'bed,' and all that surrounded him faded from my vision. "He's gone!" I exclaimed, twin feelings of regret and loss washing over me in equal parts, like a cold wave.

In a clear but quiet voice, the Shaman spoke to the Grandfather, thanking him for his trust. He then offered closing prayers to the Great Creator, Wakan Tanka Tunka Silla. I heard his voice, as from a distance, through my tears. The Shaman took me onto his lap, wiped away my tears, and rocked me back and forth in his arms, as you would a child. "Not to worry," he reassured me, "the Grandfather will be back."

And so it was. The Grandfather returned time and time again over the course of the next six or seven weeks to show us what was needed to help the People return to The Good Red Road.

Our second meeting with the Grandfather went very well. He told us he had been dreaming of how to help the People return to their true path. He asked the Shaman to do a painting of him. Within the painting, many messages would be placed, some subtle, some not at all subtle, but each of the messages would act as a trigger mechanism to the Collective Memory of the People.

When this painting was finished, the Grandfather explained, he would tell us where, how, and to whose attention it was to be sent.

The Shaman was blessed with many gifts, one of the greatest being an exceptional talent for painting. His expertise included, but was by no means limited to, oils, watercolors, acrylics, intricate line drawings, landscapes, seascapes, and portraiture.

Each detail of the birds and animals he painted was rendered with such true authenticity that the subjects appeared as though they might leap or fly from the paintings at any given moment.

Personally, I felt the Shaman's crowning glory and his true hallmark to be the powerful renditions of Native American Grandmothers and Grandfathers he so lovingly evoked from his own visions and dreams.

It is no surprise to me that the Shaman's paintings were the vehicle chosen by the Grandfather to show the People the value of a return to the old ways, the good ways of health, happiness, and harmony.

Because of the Grandfather's great vision, and his belief in the courage and receptivity of the People, we three set forth on this remarkable journey. As the journey continued to unfold, it became an Odyssey of discovery beyond anything we could have imagined. Had such a journey ever been embarked upon before? We wondered.

In one of our first meetings with the Grandfather, as is proper, each of us introduced ourselves. The Shaman and I found it difficult to understand the Grandfather's name and, finally, in exasperation, he directed us to a phonetic spelling of his name. He told us his name was Ka-tah-na-shea.

Grandfather Ka-tah-na-shea told us that he would guide us in the making of the painting. He explained that every single detail must be exactly right because, together, the details formed a cohesive 'whole' that could not readily be perceived by the conscious, but was a clear blueprint for harmony to the unconscious mind.

"Everything is a process," Grandfather explained. "Absolutely everything," he reiterated. "And the process cannot be hurried. It is imperative that each 'piece of the puzzle' fall into place at exactly the right time, in exactly the right way."

The Shaman and I looked at one another quizzically. "Grandfather Ka-tah-na-shea," the Shaman asked, "We mean no disrespect, but some of the phrases you use, such as blueprint and puzzle, are not only fairly modern, but are in no way from the Native American background. How is that possible?"

"I like to 'keep up,'" Grandfather explained. "You know the phrase, 'When in Rome, do as the Romans do?'"

This was the first of many occasions when we were to experience the joy of seeing Grandfather's ear-to-ear grin. For a moment, I thought he might burst out laughing aloud. His face was still awash with residual laughter when he replied, "Has it occurred to you that we are not speaking aloud, but mind to mind, and in English?"

Taken aback, our faces betrayed to him that the thought had not even occurred to us. Communications with Grandfather, though halting at first, quickly evolved into an easy flow, and before very long, became a rushing river of vocal thought.

We learned that Grandfather Ka-tah-na-shea, like many of his brothers, was possessed of a keen sense of wit and a ready sense of humor, which evidenced itself in a number of ways, not the least of which were occasional practical jokes. We quickly learned that the laughter was never directed at us, but with us. Grandfather looked upon laughter as a healing balm, a universal common denominator. "Humor chases away darkness, negativity, and helps to open closed minds," he explained. "No matter how difficult a situation may appear, with laughter, no problem is insurmountable."

"Like love," Grandfather Ka-tah-na-shea further expounded, "laughter is one of the great gifts Creator has given to us. Our Creator expects us to fully embrace and enjoy each and every one of the gifts that have been given to us."

Each time we visited with Grandfather, he became stronger. From his weak beginnings, when it was difficult even for him to speak, he had steadily progressed to the point where he was now sitting up. Much of his blue color had receded. His skin was now a paler shade of blue; his surroundings as well, were muted, softer.

Grandfather began to share with us the particulars of the painting, the sacred significance of it all. In our shared vision with Grandfather, we saw before us an extensive area of uniquely formed red rocks, of every shape, size, and description.

These red rocks seemed possessed of a powerful energy, appearing to glow from within. A halo of light outlined the peaks of a distant mountain range against the dark sky. Grandfather stood in a flat place atop the highest of the red rocks in a shaft of sacred light emanating from above, awash in the glow of Creator's divine revelations.

Grandfather stood, feet braced shoulder-width apart, overlooking the place where a confluence of three rivers met, though you could see but one of these rivers. Over eons of time, the now visible river had sought a serpentine path, cutting the rock away with relentless precision to evolve into a conduit for clear, free-flowing water.

As time passed, I found it difficult to restrain my curiosity and, one day, I grew bold enough to ask Grandfather to tell us about his life. "I am reluctant to speak of it," he answered. Crestfallen, I felt ashamed to have committed a breach of etiquette, however unintentional.

The Shaman, equally curious, rephrased my question in a more proper way. "Grandfather, each of us believes, as you do, that ego no longer holds a place in our lives. We have believed that for a long time—since we came to better understand what is true and what is not true. We know that an honorable man or woman is accepted by the truth evidenced by his or her actions, and by the integrity with which they live their lives. We do understand your reluctance to speak about yourself."

Pausing for breath, the Shaman continued, "Respectfully, may one ask how others in your village might have regarded you?"

Grandfather pondered but a moment. "Yes. That would be acceptable," he said slowly. "Perhaps this added insight might help you to achieve a more powerful painting. It is important that the strongest possible message be sent to the people through the painting."

"In answer to your question, some of those in my village might have regarded me as a leader. I think they respected my age." Grandfather Ka-tah-na-shea chuckled. "My people associated age with wisdom, you know. And—we have always honored our elders."

"Were you considered a chief?" I asked.

"No, I was not considered a chief." Grandfather answered, again chuckling. "Nor was I considered a holy man, or a medicine man."

"I was just a man—a man who had lived a long time, and learned some things along the way. People came to me because of that. Often, they wanted to know my thoughts about a particular situation or problem they were experiencing. So I listened to what they had to say. I offered no advice, nor did I solve their problems. They already knew the solutions to their problems when they came to see me."

"How was it that the people were helped by coming to see you, then?" the Shaman inquired.

Grandfather pondered a moment before replying, "I think the people were helped in a couple of ways. By speaking aloud about their problems, I think it helped them to see in a better way, to put things in perspective."

Grandfather Ka-tah-na-shea continued in a soft tone, as though he were thinking out loud, "When ideas, beliefs, or thoughts are kept close to the heart, they hold great power. When released, through speech, into the greatness of the universe, these same ideas, beliefs, and thoughts, with rare exceptions, become small and diluted, without power. So the problems people speak aloud are put back in their true place, and balance is restored, allowing the person to walk in a good way."

The Shaman and I nodded to one another in mute acknowledgment of the wisdom of Grandfather's words.

"Great truths spoken aloud, however," Grandfather continued, "are entirely a different matter. Great truths are rare exceptions,

172

unlike the problematic situations we discussed earlier.

"An idea whose time has come is a powerful truth indeed. Speaking about a powerful truth will not only fail to dilute that power, but, in fact, as people freely discuss the great truth, the truth itself will gain strength and power.

"These great truths have 'a life of their own' and the more they are pondered in Council, the more they are spoken of among the people, the greater and more accepted an idea becomes, until the idea becomes a substantial, ingrained power among the people."

"Would a great truth be so obvious that it would immediately be accepted by everyone?" the Shaman questioned.

"Once in a while," Grandfather continued, "that would be the case. Most times, however, an idea of this magnitude would begin slowly, building quietly by degrees until a time came when it became so prevalent, it would be discussed at great length."

"How long would these discussions take, before a consensus was reached?"

"How long would it take to reach a consensus, Nephew?" A bright smile briefly lit Grandfather Ka-tah-na-shea's face. "It took as long as it took."

A fleeting look of embarrassment crossed the Shaman's face. Observing this, Grandfather soothed, "You must remember we lived in very different times from those you live in today. Most times, we enjoyed a rhythmic flow to everyday living, both within

173

the family units and within the village as a whole.

"Today there is great difficulty from all of the stress that is evidenced. I know that your private time is very limited. Quiet thoughts and quiet moments for listening to your heart are few. Moments of contemplation are fleeting. It is hard to maintain your center, harder still to live in harmony with self and in harmony with the universal all.

"We experienced stress in our day, too, but it mostly concerned the sporadic hardship of our day to day living. Our great strength, in those days, was the gift of time. Time was our great ally.

"Necessarily, of course, there were times when we were totally engrossed in work, engaged in hunting or trading, preparing for the lean months of winter. Sometimes, we raided other tribes for horses, goods, women, or children. Occasionally, we went on the warpath to avenge a wrong done to one of our people—or all of our people. Our primary focus as warriors, however, was not so much to attack, as to be prepared for attack, to defend our families and our village.

"Still, other times were set aside in order to engage in learning. We found ourselves engrossed in teaching our young people. Much of our work, however, still left us free to think, and think we did!

"We had time to think, time to pray, time to love, and time to contemplate all things in depth.

"Some of the great joys that our Creator saw fit to give us, were the gifts of speech, thought, and free will. We gladly employed these gifts in communicating freely with one another at great length.

"Our dreams and visions were of paramount importance to us, and were often discussed for days on end, each seemingly insignificant detail examined from every possible standpoint, each possible meaning presented. To us, you see, no detail was without significance. We believed that we were part of the great tapestry of the whole and that everything that happened was with purpose, all part of Creator's plan.

"You must remember that some of our people were great orators. When a leader spoke, especially in Council, everyone listened with rapt attention—though emotions sometimes 'ran high' enough that another's speech was interrupted. This was considered 'bad manners,' however, and poorly tolerated; it was the rare exception.

"Respect for the opinions of one another was a way of learning, a way of exploring, and a way of gravitating toward a solution. In a way, our differences kept us strong, because our differences led to a path of solution and unity. Our differences lead to re-centering and harmony.

"We lived always with the heartbeat of the Mother drumming in our ears and pulsing through every fiber of our being. We lived in the surety of harmony with all living creatures, the four-leggeds, the winged ones, the crawling ones, those who inhabited the water, the Rock People, and the Tree Nations.

"At night, we looked in awe too great to describe at the multitude of the Star Nations, and remembered where we came from. We were a happy people.

"But all of that changed when the White Man came. The White Man came with weapons of great power, weapons that killed without honor from great distances, weapons that spoke death for brave warriors, weapons that destroyed our villages in short order, weapons that nearly destroyed us as a people. And yet, we fought —we fought bravely for our honor, our tribes, our families, and our way of life.

"Some of the white warriors were also very brave; some were well-intentioned and wished to make peace. But most whites did not fight like true men. Sadly, among so many of them, there was no honor. The words, even of their chiefs, could not be trusted. We never understood their methods of warfare. We never understood them as a people.

"But they came in great numbers, numbers without end. They proved to be thieves, who took the land we called home, and liars, who dishonored their own treaties. They were destroyers of the Mother and the four-legged children of the Mother.

"We had long known the whites would come one day; our Prophesies had told of their coming for so long, no one remembered when this was first known. Many of our elders saw the coming of the whites as the end of life for us, and they were right. Life as we had known it, lived it, and loved it, was forever changed.

"We called the whites the destroyers.

"In the years that followed, the forced changes that had been implemented all but forbid our way of life. Apathy and depression ruled. Disharmony became a way of life. The People fell away from The Good Red Road. They forgot the old ways. They forgot who they were. Nothing was as it had been. Nothing was as it should be.

"This loss of hope continued even into the Spirit World, the Blue World. When you first met me, my heart was crying, suffering for the people, and this suffering had made me weak. I was near true death. When a soul suffers long enough without relief, that soul will ultimately cease to exist. This is a tragedy beyond imagining, since the cessation of one single soul in all the Universe will forever change the dynamic of all that is and all that will be from this time forward.

"True death is not to be confused with 'ordinary' physical death. Death simply means we continue to work from the other side until it is time for us to be reborn again. This happens over and over again until we have attained a certain level of awareness and understanding. Then we attain true life.

"True life is not reversible, and neither is true death, for true death is the death of the soul. There could be no greater loss.

"True death of the soul would indeed be a cause for the greatest level of grieving known, for a soul is lost. A soul is lost to all eternity. The sorrow of the grieving heart will forever remain a wounded heart.

"The sufferer will not know why this is so, for he will have no conscious memory of the lost soul. We all know people like this. We know people who are never quite whole, people we have a very difficult time understanding. We have no patience with such people, for we, ourselves, have not yet attained the level of awareness and understanding necessary to feel the sufferer's terrible loss, the terrible 'gaps' in the soul of the other. Instead, we ostracize, alienate, and further cause more complete destruction and death to the wounded one.

"We must work together to help the understanding, a return to harmony within all people, for they are crying for help. Our brothers and sisters are crying for our help. Our elders and our young ones are crying for our help. Our Mother, who has suffered greatly, is crying to us for help. All of the Nations are crying to us for our help."

Grandfather Ka-tah-na-shea quietly lifted his right hand to the sky and slowly turned the palm toward us. The Red Hand!

"This is the blood of the people," Grandfather emphasized. "The blood of the people calls for a return to the Old Ways, to the ways of truth, the ways of integrity, and the ways of unity. We must become as one people, a universal tribe, celebrating our wholeness and harmony. All else will follow.

"Now, in this time, in this place, we must become more than we are. We must become more than we think we are capable of becoming. We must all become leaders. We must all become healers of one another. We must all become healers of all Nations. We must become the ones we have been waiting for."

Leadership for the People

The 'heaviness' of the day was palpable. Wires strung from nearby power lines were singing out silver against a darkly ominous sky. In the distance, lightning was erupting in seemingly random, circuitous paths across the sky. And thunder beings were speaking, becoming more vociferous as they approached. Huge bolts of lighting struck again and again into the waters of the river and the bay.

Together, the Shaman and I, anxious to be with Grandfather Ka-tah-na-shea once again, quickly walked the short distance from his truck to the house. We shivered in response to the cool contrast the drops of rain splashing over our bodies afforded. The suddenness of the cool rain meeting the searing air was already causing clouds of steam to rise from the warm pavement, and even from the grass.

We said our prayers and drifted easily, eagerly, into a deep meditation. Each of us in turn greeted the Grandfather with respect and honor, as is proper. Pleasantries were exchanged.

Only when the time seemed 'right' did the Shaman speak. "I have another question about tribal leadership," the Shaman put forth. "How did someone become a leader among the people?"

"Though correlations might be made, our people generally did not come to prominence in the same ways as your modern-day leaders. In our particular tribe, and many others, though a son *might* follow his father as a leader, there was *generally* no 'formal' line of succession, no expectation of entitlement or continuation. No family ties or influence could ensure acceptance as a leader. Leadership had to be earned.

"I suppose, in a way, leaders were 'elected.' Selected by popular acclaim, anyone aspiring to a higher station was expected to prove himself in a number of ways if he hoped to be successful in becoming a leader among the people."

"What might have inspired a person to become a leader?"

"There were a lot of aspects which might influence someone's decision. A youngster might have such regard for one of his elders that he elected to 'become just like him or her.' And if that person was recognized as a leader among the people, an almost-unconscious decision to emulate and follow in that person's footsteps might be decided. So that would be a free-will choice to become a leader.

"A choice might be made through necessity—for instance, if no one else seemed qualified to lead in a particular way, at a particular time, duty would require a responsible person to 'take charge.' This might occur if a leader were very suddenly killed, through warfare, defending his family, his village, or on a raid or a hunt.

"With no personal aspirations to advance within the tribal hierarchy, a person might be called by Creator to become a leader."

"How so?" the Shaman interjected.

Grandfather continued. "A person might feel compelled to leadership through visions, dreams, or insights. It was all part of Creator's plan—which we honored.

"You must remember that things were not as they are today. Our lives were suffused with spirituality. It is imperative that you not mistake spirituality for religion; today, people often interchange the two, or wrongly substitute one for the other.

"We who lived in those days had no word for, or understanding of, 'religion.' Religion was an alien concept to us, appearing only at the end of the free times experienced by the people.

"Religion was brought to the people by white missionaries, who had no understanding or tolerance for our spirituality. They were convinced they were 'helping us to a 'better life.'

"The missionaries wasted no time understanding us as true human beings. They perceived us to be a primitive people, lacking in sound judgment, incapable of living our own lives without help.

"Missionaries proved neither respectful nor interested enough to try to understand our way of life. The 'rules' governing every aspect of our lives were extremely complex, stemming from ancient times. 'Tried and true,' these practices for social interaction within the tribe were ways to assure the continuation of harmony.

"Structured guidelines for all aspects of tribal living prevailed. Courtship, marriage, terms of engagement in warfare, hierarchy of 'government,' warrior societies, and unwritten designs for interactive social mores were solidly in place. These time-tested guidelines had evolved over the course of many generations. It was imperative that the tribe present as a unified and purposeful 'one.' Survival itself, tenuous and fleeting, depended upon the working harmony established within the living 'core' of the people.

"The missionaries understood almost none of our ways. Nor did they care to learn. Had the missionaries taken the time and shown the respect needed to understand our values, the codes we lived by, even in small measure, they might have recognized that the religion they so fervently and self-righteously insisted on substituting for our spirituality appeared as a watered-down 'weak sister' to most of the people.

"We lived our spirituality! We lived it every day, all day, and were glad to do it. Each breath we took celebrated Creator—and celebrated all of creation—all of the time. Our spirituality encompassed the whole of our lives and was virile and active—the very center for all that we were, all that we stood for. Each breath was a tribute to Creator, powerful beyond imagination.

"Our children came to know Spirituality in their own ways, in their own time. We found our children eager to learn, and 'taught by example.' Our youth, over the course of time, came to appreciate how very central were the ways of Spiritual living. We encouraged our young ones to walk in a good way, to honor those in our community, especially the tribal elders, to do good works whenever possible, and, on all occasions, to comport themselves with dignity and pride of bearing—to be proud without living into the ego. Education, both spiritual and practical, was often placed in the capable hands of Grandparents, who gladly accepted this responsible charge.

"Community life was just that, a community living together, most times living in harmony. Like you, Creator placed us here as human beings. And like you, we occasionally embraced some of the maladies humans have always suffered—lust, greed, ambition, and avarice, to name a few.

"So we, too, were prone to weakness, irresponsibility, and other failings. In short, we humans learned hard lessons from our human frailties. But learning from mistakes is a key lesson. And in the venue of spirituality, when learning occurs, harmony is restored. Spiritual balance returns.

"One of the keystones to spirituality is the common denominator of respect—for each person, each animal, each rock, each plant, each insect—every single one of Creator's gifts."

"Grandfather," I began.

"Child, I must rest now," he sighed. "But before I leave you, I want to show you something that will be of interest to you."

Suddenly, we again 'saw' Grandfather Ka-tah-na-shea against the same backdrop as before—the red rock terrain, the dark sky, standing out in dramatic contrast against the distant mountains.

Grandfather still stood humbly, yet majestically, in a sacred shaft of light. His right hand was stretched skyward with open palm. His left arm cradled the sacred pipe.

Behind him, a prayer rug, a thunderbird bowl, a fan, a very small tobacco bowl, and three especially sacred rocks were in evidence.

The centerpiece of this sacred area was the imprint of a red hand pressed against one of the rocks, fingers spread wide and lifting to the sky in a gesture of open-handedness. We then realized that the palm of Grandfather's right hand, lifted skyward in the same attitude of trusting acceptance, was red. Only recently had Grandfather Ka-tah-na-shea pressed his palm print to the rock.

Questions flew about in my mind like a covey of startled birds. "Grandfather," I began breathlessly.

"Enough, child," Grandfather gently chided. "It is time for me to rest now."

Seeing the crest-fallen look on my face, Grandfather said, "I will be back before you know it." Looking from me to the Shaman, he added, "Then it will be time to begin painting."

And he was gone.

Momentarily, we were filled with feelings of loss at Grandfather's sudden departure, but excitement quickly 'took over' as we continued to understand the magnitude of this sacred task Grandfather had entrusted to us.

"Let's give thanks to Creator," the Shaman said.

Today Is a Good Day to Die

Today is a good day to die. Today is a good day to die. Today is a good day to die! Today is a good day to die!

What does this mean? Today is a good day to die? This simple prayer says it all. This serves as the touchstone prayer, not only to Creator, but of Creator. It is a prayer of connection to all of Creation. We become one with all the sacred energies of the universal all.

We are as brothers with all of Creator's works. We are as one with the rock nation. Each tree, each bee, each flower, each single blade of grass—become our family. Our relatives are the crawling ones, winged ones, and the four-leggeds.

As well, we are one with the Star people, and all the manifold dwellers that live within the great vault of the 'heavens.'

Today is a good day to die! In this prayer, we not only acknowledge, but accept completely and without question, the loving guidance of Great Creator, Wakan Tanka Tunka Silla.

In complete, trusting acquiescence, we turn ourselves over to our Creator.

This 'let go, let God' attitude affords us the great gift of absolute freedom. And with the gift of freedom comes the equal gift of responsibility, fueled by our free will.

The delicate balance of freedom and free will in our lives is of paramount importance, a symbiotic dance of life that evolves to make us who we ultimately become, sharing the values and intrinsic truths that we have come ultimately to represent.

Thoughts, both positive and negative, translate to energy changes—everywhere, on all levels, all of the time, culminating in universal changes. This universal understanding makes it imperative that we take responsibility for ourselves. We must walk in a good way. We must stay strongly upon the Good Red Road. We must aspire, on all occasions, to walk in beauty.

Within the sacred circle of our beliefs, the value of prayer cannot be measured. Prayer is the touchstone of our lives. For many Native Americans, it is as important as breathing. Each breath is a living reassurance that we are loved, protected, and valued. We live our lives, held securely and safely in the hand of our Creator.

Each day, the Shaman and I traveled together in our visions, and spent time in prayer, both separately and together. As was prevalent in many Native American cultures, men and women did not often pray together.

Early on in my spiritual journey, the Old Ones directed me to proper forms of prayer. I was told specifically how to pray. Each morning, arising at an early hour, the way to prayer involved cleansing—cleansing one's body, and then cleansing one's mind before going to prayers.

I was told to stand for prayers, facing the east, in honor of the return of Grandfather Sun. Each time he awakens to a new day, Grandfather Sun reminds us of one of Creator's great gifts—the ongoing reassurance of new beginnings for the ever-changing, ever-growing self.

The Old Ones specified how imperative it is to go to the quiet self within before beginning to pray. Working within each harmonious breath, with an open heart and an open mind, prayers may begin.

I was told to respectfully speak aloud in a clear, understandable voice. I was instructed not to be hesitant or shy, but, without being too loud, to 'speak up' and to clearly make known the content of my prayers.

I was told to use no personal pronouns in conjunction with self. There were to be no references to "I" or "me." These designates are considered to be words of the ego, and have no place in Native American prayer. I was told, instead, to refer to myself as This One, or sometimes more specifically as This One, Wachetecuma.

Prayers ended not with an Amen, but, instead, with a firmly spoken Aho! A period of quiet reflection sometimes followed prayer. Just as often, however, prayers were followed by a period of 'no reflection,' in which no active or passive linear thinking was entertained.

Instead, the peaceful spirit enters into a realm of spiritual comfort, and without thought or intent, immediately seeks out a place that is personally meaningful. This place most often is extremely beautiful and peaceful.

This peaceful 'being within' might have been triggered by the person's innate desire for true balance and harmony within self— or perhaps it was as simple as revisiting a place from the person's present or past lives.

When it is time, the person slowly returns to 'reality,' feeling refreshed and energized—ready for this new day, this new opportunity—to begin. Aho!

Three Rivers

We were on our way to Three Rivers. Three Rivers—the name itself sounded magical, conjuring up visions of rushing water culminating in a central confluence of singular power.

We were meeting an old friend of the Shaman's there. For some time now, we seemed to be in a place removed. My sense of hearing was acute. The sky was so bright, even with sunglasses, that it hurt my eyes. The heat waves radiating back up from the floor of the desert seemed almost tangible. I felt certain I could reach out and touch them. I was suffused with anticipation and excitement, my entire being pulsing at a higher frequency.

Throughout our journey, unseen forces appeared to guide us on all occasions—some would say it was intuition or 'a gut feeling.' It was far more than that. Each of us was keenly aware, and grateful, that our spirit guides and spirit animals were with us each step of the way.

Our objective was to find a sacred place the Shaman had visited in years past—a place of rock art, of pictographs. But we were lost. Slowly we drove up one dirt road and then down another, fighting to keep from being discouraged.

Just when we were about to give up the search, we became aware of an overwhelming scent of burning white sage. We noticed if we turned away from our destination, the scent lessened, and if we turned *toward* our destination, the scent was warm, pungent, and all pervasive.

We pulled to the side of the road and parked the truck. Defying our personal lifelong practice to honor the property of others, without hesitation, we hurriedly brushed past a 'no trespassing' sign to climb a barbed wire fence surrounding private property. Convinced that our 'mission' far surpassed the normal boundaries of behavior, we began to walk, with quickening breath, toward several adjacent, towering heaps of rocks clustered together in a loose proximity.

As we walked toward the rocks, the scent of smoking white sage was absolutely overpowering; it filled the nostrils, the mind, and the senses with a sweet, pungent, mildly acrid dry smoke. It suffused all thought, all action, as it was meant to do. We knew with a certainty that our path was true.

Once in the rocks, we climbed carefully upward. We climbed without a word being spoken, intent upon our goal. I found myself able to 'pick up' on the Shaman's thoughts and understood his cautionary message—that a single misstep might easily result in the break of an ankle, or allow for a foot to be trapped in the rocks. These fleeting concerns were dwarfed by his feeling of great excitement at meeting his friend once more. Though the Shaman's back was to me as we climbed ever upward, I could feel him smiling, anticipating with joy the reunion to come.

We climbed until we reached a point near the top. Abruptly, the Shaman made a turn and disappeared from sight! All at once, I couldn't breathe, my breath restricted by shock. Where had he gone? Had he fallen between the rocks? Was he trapped? I listened intently. Perhaps the Shaman was unable to call out to me for help. I heard only the wind singing a mysterious song, breathing off the sharp face of the rocks. Almost at once, the Shaman's head and shoulders appeared. From my vantage point, I breathed a sigh of relief.

The Shaman motioned to me, urging me to join him. I finished the climb and was surprised to look down and see the Shaman standing, shoulder-high, in a depression that was wide enough to accommodate him with room to spare.

He lifted his arms to help me down. I hesitated for a moment. Visions of snakes, lizards, spiders, and unknown terrors lurking around every rock filled my mind. The Shaman grinned at me and shook his head.

I suddenly felt foolish. Without another thought, I leaned forward into his waiting arms. The heat of the day was suddenly replaced with the cool airflow emanating from the shaded rock corridors. It felt wonderful.

At first it was hard to see in the shaded areas, but in a very short time, I could see quite clearly, and was surprised to see before me, a free-form corridor winding through rocks, which were not only as big as small buildings, but as small as a grain of sand.

The corridor we followed doubled back on itself several times, until we came upon a table-like rock surface, flanked on all sides by higher formations.

"Here we are," the Shaman said. "Take a look around."

I took a look around. Pictographs! Ancient rock art! I was stunned. "Wow!" I intoned softly. Slowly, I turned in a circle, visually examining each unique pictograph "drawing," one by one. I was amazed at how complex, how intricate, were the designs.

The power of the feelings that were loosed within my conscious—and unconscious being—defied description. I literally felt like a different person. Everything was sharply delineated.

I felt "light-headed' and 'light-bodied." I literally felt as though I were floating a few inches off the ground.

I saw in my "mind's eye" as though I were seeing myself from a different vantage point. How had I "flown" through the corridors to this place, this time?

Abruptly, I felt the full impact of my body. The quick intake of air through my nostrils was almost hurtful in its intensity. As my lungs expanded, I shuddered with the sudden release of such concentrated energy. In my mind's eye, I saw this energy "shoot out," following an extremely rapid series of "lines" coursing throughout my body—in no more time than it would take to snap your fingers. Idly, I wondered if these "lines" were in fact, veins or arteries.

"Fascinating, aren't they?"

"What?" I said, still lost in my thoughts and feelings.

The Shaman grinned. "The pictographs—they're fascinating, don't you agree?"

"Oh, yes—to say the least," I agreed, struggling to focus. "How did you ever find them, hidden way back here? You couldn't possibly have seen them from the road. You wouldn't have been able to see them from outside this rock formation, either." Almost as an afterthought, I asked, "Who do you think created this artwork?"

"Whoa!" the Shaman laughed. "Your questions will soon be answered. Why don't we sit down?"

The Shaman motioned to the tabletop rock we were standing on. We seated ourselves cross-legged on the smooth, welcoming coolness of the rock surface.

"How did the pictographs get here?" I persisted.

"This is the site of an ancient east-west trade route used for centuries by peoples who lived long before the Anasazi. Information about the pre-Anasazi people is almost non-existent; unlike later tribes whose word-of-mouth history has been preserved at least in part, much of the way people lived in that pre-Anasazi period has remained largely undiscovered.

I was mystified. "How do you know that?"

The Shaman thought for a moment, as though carefully choosing his words, "I know about it because of a journey I was led to pursue several years ago. It was a complex journey that unfolded a little at a time until at last I arrived here in much the same way as you and I were led here today."

"But..." I started to interject.

"Shh!" the Shaman placed his index finger gently across his lips, indicating a need for silence. He cocked his head as if listening, and began to smile.

Seeing I was about to speak again, he shook his head and said, "Listen."

I closed my eyes, the better to listen intently, and at first I heard nothing—nothing, that is, except for the musical sound of laughter—the laughter of two men! The infectious laughter of the Shaman mixed with the quiet laughter of another man.

My eyes snapped wide open. The Shaman and a much smaller man stood facing each other, right hands clasping one another's forearms in greeting, left hands firmly gripping right shoulders. Though I had never seen this form of greeting before, it was clearly 'the handshake of days gone by.'

The two men then embraced one another as brothers and seated themselves, including me in their small circle. The Shaman's friend smiled in welcome. His calloused hands were surprisingly gentle, as he took both my hands in his. "My name is Echecha." Almost as an afterthought, he advised, "You may call me Grandfather, or Grandfather Echecha."

"Thank you, Grandfather. I am called Wachetecuma."

"You are the friend of my friend."

"Yes," I agreed, "I am the friend of your friend." Gracefully, gently, Grandfather Echecha guided me through one of the forms of proper address from ancient times. Instinctively, I understood the pivotal role played by this orderly ritual—this 'dance' of mutual respect.

"Then I am your friend, also," Echecha intoned.

"And you are my friend." Overcome with the emotion of the moment, I realized my eyes were suddenly filled with tears. I was overwhelmed, completely awed by the sacredness of the moment. I felt, as I have so often before, that each moment in time connects to all others, and in that moment, I lived again through the ancient pulse of the Mother.

At length, I lifted my head to see before me the open, approving faces of the Shaman and the Grandfather, blessing me with their smiles, their openness, and their acceptance.

Without a word, the Shaman produced a bit of tobacco for each of us. We stood and each of us, in turn, offered this tobacco to the four directions. Taking my cues from the men, I seated myself, following the offering.

The Shaman produced a soft leather pouch from which he carefully lifted a red flannel bundle. Sprinkles of tobacco were loosed as he carefully opened the flannel, and I saw that he was holding the bowl of a sacred pipe. This he handed to Grandfather Echecha while he removed the stem of the pipe from its wrapping. Nodding his thanks to Grandfather Echecha, the Shaman then fitted stem to bowl, completing the sacred pipe.

"Grandfather, will you do the honors?" the Shaman asked, handing the pipe and a small leather pouch containing a traditional 'tobacco' mix to him.

I watched as Grandfather withdrew a flint, a second stone, and a medium-sized open-faced seashell from a pouch at his waist. He also produced a small twist of grass, which he laid aside. Reaching again into the pouch, he withdrew the barest handful of crushed leaves and grass.

Carefully placing the crushed leaves and grass in the shell, he struck the flint against the other stone, producing a spark, which immediately ignited the grass and leaves in the shell. Nurturing this small flame, Grandfather Echecha soon lit the pipe with the twist of smoking grass.

Following Grandfather Echecha's lead, we both stood as he lifted the lit pipe once more to the four directions, to softly offer a prayer. Having smoked the pipe once around, Grandfather motioned for us to be seated.

And so we smoked—and time stood still.

Presently, the pipe was 'smoked out,' and was lovingly disassembled and carefully 'put away' once more.

Grandfather examined the residue of the burned grass and leaves still in the shell. Satisfied that they were 'out,' he lifted the shell to the sky, allowing the meager remains to fly forth on the wind. Then, the flint stone and 'striking-against' stone, along with the seashell, were carefully returned to Grandfather's pouch. Only then did he speak.

"Good," Grandfather Echecha said. "How is it with you, my friend?"

"It goes well, Grandfather. The journey continues to unfold in a good way. I am learning to read sign better than before."

Grandfather Echecha laughed. "Yes, it becomes easier to read sign as your journey continues. In time, though, you will learn to stop reading sign. Instead, you will allow the sign to speak, and the way will become clear to you.

"All signs lead to the Good Red Road, and when the way becomes clear to you, the Good Red Road will flow like a river before you. Your way will be true—and joyous!"

The Shaman and I contemplated Grandfather Echecha's words in a relaxed silence, a silence of the soul.

At length, Grandfather Echecha said, "I see the bowl of your pipe comes from the Anishinabe North Country."

"Yes," the Shaman confirmed. "I was advised by the keeper of the sacred rock that one small piece of stone would call to me. This single piece I was given permission to gently carve from the face of Mother Rock."

"That is indeed a great honor," Grandfather agreed.

"The Shaman carved into the pipe bowl some of his totem animals," I volunteered, "and symbols, as well."

"Those ones," Grandfather explained to me, "those totem animals have lived long and willingly within the sacred stone. Their dreams told them of the Shaman's coming. They waited patiently to be discovered. The Shaman's coming, they knew, would help them to come forth in a tangible way, to inspire all those who gaze upon their likenesses while smoking the sacred pipe."

To the Shaman, he said, "You have done well. You have listened and heard the totem animals calling to you from within the stone. Those ones were glad that you understood the balance represented by honoring the on-going union between them, and the sacred stone." Grandfather reiterated.

"Grandfather, the home of this sacred red stone is far from this place. How is it that you know of the pipe stone?" the Shaman inquired.

A fleeting smile crossed the Grandfather's face. "The mountain from which this stone originates," he explained, "is the only place where this stone can be obtained—anywhere! It is the *only* place this stone has chosen to live.

"The keepers of this pipe stone have been very carefully chosen as guardians of this sacred trust. They dedicate their lives to keeping the trust. They live all their lives as brothers with the mountain, from whose belly they bring forth this life-affirming gift Creator has bestowed upon certain people. These generations of guardians, father to son, to son, to son, to son, to son, ongoing, must remain unbroken. The guardianship is a blood trust that only a few families have been honored with."

The Shaman and I were quiet, contemplating all this.

Grandfather Echecha, using a familiar form of address, turned toward the Shaman. "But to answer your question, Nephew, I know about the sacred pipe stone and the sacred mountain from which it comes because, as a trader, I met one of the Guardians of that place."

As an after-thought, he added, "In the 'old' days, I met them."

203

"Grandfather," I made so bold as to ask, "Would you tell us about your life as a trader? How did you become a trader?"

Stretching his legs out before him and leaning back against a 'wall' abutting the rock 'tabletop' where we found ourselves, Grandfather settled himself more comfortably. The Shaman and I did the same.

"In answer to your question," Grandfather said to me, "I did not become a trader. I was born a trader."

"But where was your village, your home?" I persisted.

"We *were* the village; we were a traveling village. As far back as anyone in our band could remember—there was no 'home' village. Home was wherever we were. All of us, men, women and children, traveled together from one place to another, trading as we went."

"How many of you were there?" the Shaman wanted to know.

"Our numbers changed all the time," Grandfather explained. "We were as many as fifty sometimes, but when there was trouble, sometimes we numbered no more than fifteen or twenty."

"What kind of trouble?" I wanted to know.

"In hard times, there might be serious storms that caused floods, or too much snow, or drought, thus restricting the ability to travel, and to trade freely. Yet, other times, we were subject to unexpected situations that demanded quick resolution.

"Large predators abounded in the land then, and were a threat to adults and children alike. We did our best to fend them off, but were not always successful.

"Starvation was an enemy lurking just around the corner, especially in lean trade years."

"What about disease, Grandfather?" I interjected.

"Widespread disease among the people is a fairly recent phenomenon," Grandfather related quietly. "Disease seemed to coincide with the arrival of the outsiders. Before that time, the people were mostly strong and hardy.

"The job of healers in those days was to keep the people healthy. Since disease was thought to be brought about by the disharmony of spirit, medicine people were charged with restoring balance to the afflicted party."

"How did they do that, Grandfather?"

"Some medicine people were very gifted in understanding the uses for a variety of herbs, roots, leaves, mosses, berries, and barks. Others were gifted surgeons and were able not just to set an arm or a leg, but on occasion, they successfully performed complex operations, such as brain surgery.

"Yet others of the medicine people practiced more ancient medicine, such as hollow bones healing, or what you might think of as 'energy' healing.

"All of our healers, each of our medicine men and women, devoted their lives to honoring their craft. Most discovered an affinity for healing at an early age and, with the permission of their parents, would go to live in the lodge of the medicine man or woman to develop healing skills. From that time forward, the child would live in a world of learning to heal, a world suffused with hands-on medicine.

"Medicine people were set apart and greatly honored. Medicine men and women were cared for by others in the tribe. They did not go out to hunt or make weapons. They neither constructed their own lodges or garments, nor did they ordinarily cook.

"Because food, clothing, and housing were provided for tribal healers, they were free to pursue their dreams, visions, and spiritual quests at length.

"Medicine people, along with the help of children, also spent time gathering and processing herbal medicines. Most of the medicines were seasonal and needed to be harvested at just the right time. Some medicines were to be found only in a limited location, sometimes requiring extensive travel.

"The life of the medicine person was a life of complete dedication to the people. We felt blessed to have them living among us, caring for us. Most medicine people liked to walk in quiet ways. We honored and respected their privacy. But always, we looked to them for guidance, and when they spoke, we cherished the wisdom of their words."

A comfortable pause ensued as the Shaman and I digested this information.

"During your travels, were you ever set upon by other tribes?" the Shaman asked.

"This seldom happened," Grandfather Echecha explained. "It happened more in the beginning when our people first began to establish a trade route. There was an understood territorial imperative at work between different bands of people. One tribe was known to live in one place, and their neighbors to live in another area. Trouble began when one of these groups, whether unwittingly or knowingly, crossed these invisible boundary lines.

"War with your neighbors was a way of life in those days. It was traditional and long-standing, and, in general, was not meant to eradicate your neighbors from the face of the earth, but rather to maintain a certain level of balance of power within the tribes. In a strange way, war created a means of maintaining harmony between the tribes.

"Travel was made arduous in those days because the medicine animal called horse had not yet come to live among the people. We were not nearly as mobile as we became in later years. Until the horse came, all our trade goods, all our necessities for living, had to be carried on our backs. As soon as a child was able to walk, the smallest child 'wore' a small pack on his or her own back. The children looked forward to the day when they were considered 'big enough' to carry a pack. They were anxious to prove themselves. They were proud of the responsibility entrusted to them."

"But we were not without helpers," Grandfather smiled. "We were called Wolf Clan. There were no wolves on our trade routes, which were far to the south, but stories of our people were told of another time when we lived in the cold country and, over the course of time, migrated south—and stayed south. And with us came our friends, the wolves. No one knows how these wolves came to live among us, but live among us they did—in significant numbers.

"We looked upon the wolves as sacred helpers. Young wolves, like small children, were entrusted with small backpacks. Adult wolves often pulled goods-laden travois for long distances with little apparent effort. Occasionally, if one of us, because of wounds or injuries, was unable to walk, wolves pulled that person on a travois. When this happened, the wolves only pulled for short distances when one of their brothers replaced them in harness.

"Our brothers also alerted us to the presence of predators, and often went to battle with those predators to protect the people. Some of the wolf people gave up their lives in this way. They were very brave.

"The wolf people were still wild creatures, and yet, they were not. They were free to stay with the people or not. Not one of the people would harm one of the wolf people. We considered them a part of our tribe. Most wolves bonded with a single person, usually a child, when both were young; it was a mutual choosing. Child and wolf seemed to recognize one another at an early age, and gravitated toward one another to the exclusion of all others.

"Some of these 'wolf children' lived faithfully with a particular wolf for the entire life spans of one another, accepting other duties and responsibilities only after the death of their dearest companion.

"Without our asking, the wolf hunted for us; we thanked him and were glad. The land here was filled with long-limbed, fast running hares, which avoided our snares and arrows with relative ease. But these hares had little success in outrunning the wolf people and, seeing this, gave of themselves for the people—and to the wolves. So we shared all with one another. It was a happy union.

"Because we wished to present an image of peaceful neutrality to all people, open to trade with everyone, we traveled upon the Mother in a slow and open way, moving from one tribal area to another. Unlike most tribal units, we posted no guards. And except for the purpose of finding good water-site camping areas, we sent forth no scouts. Such was not the case with our wolf brothers, however.

"It was the natural way of the wolf brothers to continually send out scouts and post guards. What the wolf scouts and guards learned, they relayed to their wolf child, and that child would then alert the elders when others were approaching the camp how many were coming and what the general mood among the strangers appeared to be. The wolf and the wolf child were often seen staring intently into one another's eyes. In this way, they communicated, and their communications were true."

"What preparations were made when the wolf brothers reported an unfriendly group approaching?"

"We waited. If we were 'on the move,' we made camp in preparation for welcoming these strangers. If we were already in camp, we prepared food to welcome the newcomers."

"You didn't arm yourselves?" the Shaman pressed.

"No," Grandfather Echecha smiled. "What weapons we carried were for hunting and to trade. Most of our food came from trade. This was a way of acting in 'good faith,' to let others know that we were a peaceful people, coming to greet them without fear."

"So you were not warriors?"

"Do not be fooled by stereotypes, Nephew. We were *all* warriors—men, women, and children alike. We were *peaceful* warriors. It is far more difficult to face up to an armed 'enemy' without weapons than to meet in combat, each bent on prevailing over one another."

"How did you protect yourselves then?"

"We met potential enemies with the twin weapons of welcome and respect. Most times, we were able to 'disarm' our 'enemies' with friendship."

"But didn't anyone ever attack your group and just take your trade goods?" the Shaman asked.

"Yes, this happened a few times. Some of those we hoped to trade with even killed some of us," Grandfather related sadly. "There were few secrets in the mountains, in the desert areas, or on the plains in those days, however; when it was learned that we traders had been attacked, other tribes would quickly intervene. They helped us by first tending to our wounded and making sure we had food and shelter. But most important of all, they quickly restored the balance of power by exacting retribution upon the offending tribe.

"Everyone recognized that, though we might be killed and our goods taken from us, trade in that area would cease, and no more goods would be forthcoming. It was to the benefit of all the tribes that active trade be not only allowed to continue, but also encouraged.

"Within a few years of establishing our trade route, almost everyone was friendly. Sometimes, they were too friendly," Grandfather Echecha joked. "Sometimes, when we were camping in a particular place, occasionally a young man who came to trade would find himself hopelessly entranced by one of our young women. If the young woman evinced interest, a bride price would be struck and she would leave our group to marry and live among the man's people."

"Did the young men who married women from your group ever leave their tribes and come to live with you?"

"Yes, that sometimes happened," Grandfather mused, "but more often, our young women left to marry into other tribes."

"Maybe it 'evened out' in the long run," I ventured.

"Perhaps so," Grandfather replied. "Some of the children who resulted from these unions returned to our people to travel and live with their grandparents, learning to become traders. Many of these grandchildren traveled with us for the length of time it took to complete a circuit. Eventually, most returned to the village of their birth, but once in awhile, the child who came to the people never again returned to live with his or her tribe. Whatever the decision, it was solely the free will choice of the child."

"But," I interjected, "surely the parents of the child objected to his leaving them?"

"No! Never would the parents object." Pausing but a moment, Grandfather continued, "We believe that the true path of any human being is the business of that person—that person alone. To interfere or to try to alter the path of any person is considered wrong. We do not have the right to interfere in the free will decision of another. To do so would not only dishonor that individual, but our Creator, as well."

Grandfather took a breath before continuing. "The upside to these trader and tribal intermarriages was that even when one of our people went to live with another tribe, we were able to visit them every few years when our trade route carried us near to their village."

The Shaman looked incredulous. "Your trade route took several years to complete?"

212

"Oh, yes. Our travels always took several years," Grandfather reiterated.

"The route varied, depending on circumstances." Grandfather continued. "Weather was a big factor. For instance, if drought were a problem on a particular year, understanding that the tribes would have moved to a more congenial location, we would, likewise, alter our route.

"Sometimes, if an extensive war involving a big tribal area were involved, we changed our route." Grinning, Grandfather continued, "Tribes following the war trail have little interest in trading. And we had no interest of being 'caught in the middle' of a particular conflict. We jealously protected our neutrality.

"Mostly, though, we traveled from the Big Water, where Grandfather Sun sleeps, to the big river, where Grandfather begins each day. We have heard that the big river divides the land in two halves. We have followed this Grandfather River to the place of his birth, where he is a small river, to his destination, where he has grown to be a giant.

"There were a lot of tribes living in harmony with Grandfather River. It was on one of these trips that we left the Grandfather's side and went inland to find the sacred pipestone."

"Grandfather, when you were traveling, did you trade in the villages?" the Shaman inquired.

"No," Grandfather quickly replied. "Our trading took place

away from the villages; in fact, we seldom knew exactly where the villages were located. Once in awhile, when our route carried us near to a village, scouts would ride out and politely redirect us to a 'better' trading place away from the village.

"This was a way of keeping the villages safe."

"But Grandfather," I interjected, "surely you were no threat to the tribes. Clearly your way of traveling in such a slow and open way was reassurance enough for any tribe. They could see you were unarmed and that you came in friendship."

"True enough," Grandfather agreed. "But that was not the point."

Seeing our puzzled faces, he continued. "You must remember that in those days, as we spoke of before, understood tribal boundaries were honored, and the tribes were often at war with one another. Because of this, no tribe asked us to their village."

I remained quizzical.

"As we traveled, we acted as messengers, bringing news from one area to another. Understandably, the tribes did not want us to know the layout of their villages, their population, or what their defense strength might be."

"Didn't they trust you?" I asked indignantly.

"Yes, they trusted us. But they trusted human nature more. They understood that an unintentional slip of the tongue could spell disaster for their people. We knew that, and we honored their way.

"And they respected us for understanding the importance of trading away from the villages. When their scouts appeared, it was not long before members of the tribe would approach, bringing not only trade items, but food to prepare and share with us, as well. If we had been welcomed into their villages, a feast would have been prepared for us, and this was their way of welcoming us."

"What if you had a daughter who wanted to marry into a tribe? Wouldn't you be asked into a village then?" I persisted.

"No. If I had given permission for marriage to my daughter, it would have been because I saw that the man she wanted to marry was an honorable human being. And I respected her choice."

The Shaman nodded approvingly. Each of us was quiet for a spell.

"How long did your people travel in this way?" the Shaman asked.

"We traveled in this way for a long time—no one could remember how long we did this—hundreds of years in modern time measurement, for sure."

"Why did you stop trading?" the Shaman pressed.

"Our people kept trading right into the early modern times," Grandfather Echecha mused, "but when the medicine animal, which you call horse, came to live among us, everything changed. For the first time, tribes could travel far, and they could travel fast. They no longer needed us to carry goods to them; they rode out to trade for themselves.

"After awhile, some of the tribes gathered to trade at appointed times in appointed places. In recent times, these gatherings included others—some of them from far away, to the north. These 'north' traders were good men. They were strong men who liked to eat, and laughed a lot. We could not understand their tongue, but talked to them in sign.

"Others, who were not good men, soon followed. Those who followed were as numerous as the stars. They filled the prairies, the mountain country, the high plains, and the deserts. They filled these places and still they came. They assailed the senses."

"What manner of men were these?" the Shaman wanted to know.

With a small sigh, Grandfather answered, "It was our misfortune to learn what manner of men these were. These men, we were to learn, wanted to destroy the very essence of our being as a people, and they very nearly succeeded.

"Finally, they thought the people were sufficiently 'subdued.' They thought we had become 'good Indians,' so they lost interest in us. They underestimated the yearning we bore for our way of life, which was so balanced and harmonious. They failed to realize that the pride of a people living into their truth can never be subdued by mere acts of cruelty and atrocity."

"And so it was with the people, Nephew. So it was with the people."

The End of the World

When I was seven years old, I was told in strictest confidence by a neighbor girl that the world would end that very day! Clara's words were further reinforced by adult conversations I overheard.

"Yes, they swear by all that's holy," Mother's lady friend intoned over coffee.

"I heard it on the radio this morning," Mother put in.

"And there's an article about it in the morning paper," a third female voice added.

A stunned silence followed. I listened quietly, intently, from the hallway. I did not want to give myself away. Mother took a dim view on eavesdropping.

"What should we do?"

"I don't think there is much we can do."

"Well, I guess we could pray."

"Something like this really makes you stop and think, doesn't it?

"Maybe we should tell our husbands."

"I don't know what they could do about it."

More silence followed. I heard the sound of a chair scraping the floor as one of the ladies stood to leave. "Well, that ironing won't do itself. Thanks for the coffee."

"I need to get into the garden before it gets too hot. The weeds are taking over. Ladies, I enjoyed it."

"You're always welcome," I heard Mother say. "Maybe we can get together for coffee later in the week."

The sound of laughter erupted suddenly from the kitchen. "Let's hope so."

More laughter followed. "Oh, my sides hurt!" one of the ladies gasped.

"I have tears running down my face," another put in.

A muffled, "I can't stop laughing."

"Well…"

As a new wave of laughter followed, I made good my escape. I had a lot to think about. I sat on the bed in my room mulling over all that I had just heard. Obviously, I had overheard information of staggering proportions. The reactions my mother and her friends experienced seemed confusing and contradictory to me. From my hidden listening post, I had been privy to adult emotions so laced with apprehension and disbelief that they were all but palpable. And yet they were laughing. What did it all mean?

After further deliberation, I knew what to do. Quickly, I made my bed, straightened my room, and dressed. Then I went next door to my little brother's room and made sure his bed was made, his room 'picked up,' and that he was dressed.

Mother called out from the kitchen, "Kids, breakfast is ready. Get washed up, now." The light coming through the open window bathed the kitchen in a warm glow. A gentle morning breeze brought a momentary shiver as my brother and I turned our attention to bowls of steaming oatmeal glazed with cinnamon and sugar, glasses of cold milk, and raisin toast.

"I see your beds are made," Mom said. "After breakfast, you can run out and play. I don't have any chores for you this morning and I need the kitchen to do the ironing."

Our kitchen was neither large nor small, but when the ironing board was set up, it seemed to fill the entire area not taken up by the table and chairs. And Mother needed room to move around the board freely.

Ironing was a real chore in those days. There were no steam or spray irons, just moderately heavy irons that were plugged into an electric outlet. Garments to be ironed were usually 'sprinkled,' sometimes with rainwater, sometimes with well or tap water. The garments were then rolled up so the moisture was evenly distributed before ironing, thus ensuring moderately wrinkle-free 'finished' garments, which were then carefully arranged on hangers.

The vital challenge, back then, was to get the temperature of the iron 'just right.' The ironing had to be finished before 'drying out' occurred. Too little or too much moisture on a garment guaranteed scorching or wrinkling.

Sometimes, sprinkled clothing was put in the fridge to keep it cool and damp until time to iron it. That way, several garments could be sprinkled on the kitchen table at one time, thus expediting the process.

So, while Mother went through setting up for ironing in the kitchen, my brother and I went out to play. My brother quickly became engrossed with his bulldozers and trucks.

I sat down on the front porch, filled with excitement. I sat there all day.

"I wonder what it will be like," I thought. "I wonder what the end of the world will be like." The early morning temperature was still slightly cool. Not really uncomfortable, but, every once in awhile, an involuntary 'shudder' would pass through my body. It was a delightful crisp morning.

Hours passed. Mid-morning arrived, bringing warmer temperatures.

"Do you want to play?" my brother asked.

"No, I can't," I replied. "You go on ahead."

I didn't think it would be right to tell my little brother I was waiting for the end of the world. He might be worried. He was too little, I decided.

"Ok, then," he said. "I'm going to the back yard."

I briefly considered whether or not to ask him to stay with me. I was protective of my brother, always making sure he was safe.

No need to worry him, I thought. "Holler through the back screen door and tell Mom you're in the back yard, okay?"

"Okay," the reply drifted back to me. He was already half way around the house.

"Hey," I called out, "what are you going to do back there."

"Bulldoze in the sandbox, that's what!" was his irritated reply.

223

"Good, then. Have fun," I yelled back, knowing he would stay in the sandbox and not wander off and get into trouble. Brother 'loved' his bulldozer and would play with it happily for hours on end. He was totally focused, intent on moving the sand from one place to another, and back again.

On the front porch, I continued my reverie. "I wonder if it'll hurt," I thought. "I wonder if the end of the world will hurt.

"Will it be like a big storm, where there's a lot of thunder and lightening?

"Maybe it'll be like that story where the sky falls. What would it be like if the sky did fall? That couldn't be a good thing." I decided.

"I hope Brother and I still get to be with Mom and Dad," I worried. Briefly, my eyes filled with tears. "We wouldn't want to be without Mom and Dad."

Thoughts raced through my mind so fast that I could hardly think them before they were gone. This end of the world business wasn't easy.

"I wonder how we'll know when it happens."

The day was heating up dramatically now. I moved back on the porch to sit with my back against the side of the house. The siding on the house was warm against my back. The heat of it felt so good. I felt so drowsy, so completely relaxed, basking in the warmth of the sun. "Maybe everything will be alright," I thought. "Maybe the world won't end."

"Wake up!" a soft voice came from afar. "Wake up now." With difficulty, I struggled to return to consciousness. "Is it over?" Has the world ended?" I asked.

"What?" Mother laughed. "You just had a dream, that's all.

"What are you doing, sleeping out here? Are you feeling all right? Are you sick?"

Not quite awake, I answered, "Sick, no. I'm not sick." I was irritated at this rude awakening.

Mother was rapidly losing patience with me. "Well, wake up, then, and come in for lunch."

"What will I miss if I go in for lunch?" I asked myself.

It was a moot point. I knew this was a losing battle for me. Lunch was inevitable. Lunch was going to happen, whether the world ended or not. I sighed. "I'll be right there, Mother," I promised.

"Right this minute," Mother said. It was her 'don't cross me' voice.

"Okay," I said. "I'm coming."

Mom held the screen door for me. Obediently, I slipped past

her into the relative coolness of the house. It felt good. "Wash up," she ordered.

The hand pump was mounted solidly to the heavy wooden kitchen counter at the edge of the sink. It was secured to the counter with four big bolts. Quickly, I pumped just enough water into the hand basin placed in the kitchen sink to wash my hands and face. I patted my face dry and dried my hands on a small towel Mother had placed on the counter. The towel smelled good, like fresh air and sunlight.

That done, I carefully picked up the basin, pushed open the screen door, and walked down the back porch stairs, out to the fence line, where I 'threw' the water in the basin over the fence. Every now and again, if my hands or the basin were still wet, the basin would fly out of my hands, as if it had a mind of its own, to land on the other side of the fence. On the rare occasions when this happened, Mother was not pleased.

Naturally, the basin had to be retrieved and cleaned up immediately to be returned to the kitchen sink. This was not a happy event; it involved my spending time alone in my room, 'rethinking my position.' It was a boring and time-consuming event that might better be used in play. After I had 'thrown' the basin over the fence a couple of times, I determined to never again allow it to slip from my hands.

Our home had no inside plumbing. We had no bathroom, no bathtub, and no shower. We were lucky to have the hand pump in the kitchen that brought water from the well into the house.

Walking back to the house, I couldn't help but wonder if I had missed anything while I was asleep. Had I missed anything while I was washing up? Would I miss anything while I was eating lunch? I dreaded to think the world might come to an end while I was eating lunch and I might miss it. I didn't want to miss anything. But I was hungry. Lunch wouldn't take long, I reasoned. Still, I worried...

That event happened more than fifty years ago. And to my great chagrin, the world did not end that day. But it might have! I believe that single experience provided yet another important step in my spiritual journey.

That long-ago day, as I waited expectantly for the world to end —first in the crispness of morning, followed by the drowsy warmth of noontime, and finally ending my front-porch sojourn, by watching a spectacular sunset at day's end, I experienced a fleeting sense of disappointment. The absolutes of the world could not always be depended upon, I realized, my concern quickly lost, as the first fireflies of the evening made a tentative appearance. Tonight, I vowed to myself, I would catch more fireflies than my brother.

That is the first time I was aware of experiencing abstract thought. Later years would find me indulging in freethinking on all occasions, often sitting up into the small hours of the morning with my friends, presenting and rehashing our various personal and philosophical ponderings.

I believe that day I learned not only to live in what a friend describes as 'the infinite moment,' but to live also in the past, present and future as one; in short, to truly appreciate the immensity of 'the big picture.'

Each day since that time, and often several times each day, I reinvent myself. I adapt to meet whatever changing conditions present. Usually, this occurs without my thinking about it, or even being aware of it, though sometimes it is a conscious decision to change. I believe everyone experiences these changes, to varying degrees. From my standpoint, human beings are among the most resilient, adaptable mutants ever to grace this planet. And our mutations are ongoing and never-ceasing.

The world was going to end, 'they' said, in 2012—on December 21—according to the ancient Mayan Calendar.

Many believed this was to be an actual catastrophic event, culminating in the destruction of all life on earth, and perhaps Mother Earth, herself.

In my 'end of the world' scenario, perhaps catastrophic events will occur, perhaps not. What I feel will occur is an end to the 'world as we know it.' I see a necessity to return to simplicity and spirituality—in all aspects of our lives. I feel we have a great need to 'return to our centers.'

As a people, we have traveled far from our spiritual underpinnings, far from feelings of harmony and well-being. And we are suffering from this separation from Spirit. 'My' end of the world does not see the destruction of all mankind. 'My' end of the world sees a rebirth into a higher dimension of being, where we human beings take responsibility for ourselves, where we hold ourselves accountable to our God and one another, and all of the other nations we share this good earth with—to name a few, the tree nations, rock nations, four-leggeds, winged ones, swimming ones—ALL NATIONS!

The Mayan prophecy predicted the end of the world in 2012. So, too, have many other 'end of the world' predictions been forecast throughout history—and failed to materialize. We therefore need to work toward fulfilling our own prophecy. As set forth in a long-ago forecasted prophecy, "we have thought we were living in the eleventh hour. But this is not so—we are in the hour. Now is the hour."

Infinity Revisited

Infinity—what does it mean? To comprehend infinity, we must first understand the meaning of finite. Finite is used to describe measurable limits. Finite is to have definite or determinable boundaries or limitations.

At the opposite end of the spectrum, we have infinite, or infinity, which is described as the quality of the unlimited extent of time, space, or quantity. We human beings believe ourselves to be the only life form on the planet able to contemplate infinity. And this may be true. Or not true.

Yet there are much older beings than we humans living on the planet. Reason would dictate that the nation of tree people, some of whom are hundreds of years old, would have a greater probability of understanding infinity.

But we are a brash people. We believe that we are the lords of the universe and, in some ways, we are, but being lords of the universe brings big responsibilities—to begin with, care of the Mother, and care of one another. Sadly, we quite often fall short of living up to these obligations. Our tree brothers are steadfast, however, in their co-dependence and dedication to the Mother. We brash ones have forgotten that we are indeed co-dependent with the Mother, that a successful union between us is of such an intertwining that the success of one requires the success of the other.

Some of us have become so desensitized to our status that we believe we *are* the lords of the universe, lords over the Mother and all who dwell in tandem with her. Many no longer believe in God, by whatever definition we so define a Supreme Being, or higher power.

How is that possible? Not to believe in God?

How is it possible that the configuration of a single fingerprint belongs to only one person in the world, and to that one person alone?

How is it possible that a single snowflake, while similar, is never reproduced in the identical configuration?

Much of our uniqueness is not yet understood. For instance, it would be interesting to know if a fingerprint that exists today had EVER existed before in all of history.

And for those who believe in reincarnation, would one of our ancestors have carried a fingerprint identical to our own print?

A documented succession of Dali Lamas has existed for thirteen generations. Widely held belief is that the Dali Lamas, in each of the thirteen reincarnations, is the same spirit, the same soul, but more advanced in each successive lifetime.

Or if maybe millions of years ago, a snowflake fell somewhere on the Great Plains that would today be identical to a snowflake falling in my back yard right this minute.

In the arena of similarities, like snowflakes and fingerprints, I understand that no two ear prints are alike. Why is this not widely known? Perhaps because, unlike fingerprint technology, which is acknowledged as proof in solving crimes, very few ear prints are left at the scene of a crime.

But when you think of ears, think of seashells. Many of the modern day configurations of seashells date back millions of years —in the exact same pattern. Or do they? Are seashell configurations as unique as a fingerprint, no two exactly alike?

All of which brings us back to infinity. How would you describe infinity? We humans tend to 'think in the box.' If we are to truly advance and be recognized as a universal power, we need to learn not just to think outside the box, but to rid ourselves of the box entirely. We must begin to think in a new way, a universal way, if you will. We need to learn to think on a grander scale than anything we can imagine if we are to continue and thrive as a species.

To gain perspective, there is even an infinity setting on our more sophisticated cameras, a big picture setting, if you will. How can we truly understand infinity when we continually relegate our thinking to such narrow confines?

Our watchword might well be 'imagine.' Imagine what? Imagine how? The how is easy. Close your eyes and breathe. Send all thoughts from your mind, relax, and allow yourself to become aware. Awareness comes sometimes in a rush, but, more often, in small and digestible pieces of information drifting into your consciousness, almost without your knowing it. And like a small seed, given enough time, enough pieces of information gather together into a giant collective of information—which in no way approaches the concept of infinity.

But you are drawing a tiny bit closer to understanding and being able to tap into the collective consciousness of our species. If this sounds far-fetched to you, take a moment to think about how your life has developed.

Throughout your life, from time to time, the question has been posed to you, "How do you know that?" And you answered, "I don't know; I just know." Imagine.

Infinity is a state of being.

Infinity is not what we perceive to be the universe we know, but rather the universes we know exist beyond what we can see.

You might say that infinity is the whole of what we cannot possibly imagine. But what if we could...what if we could... imagine.

Remember, the hour *is* now!

To Fix or Not To Fix

To fix or not to fix—that is the question. That has always been the question when people look about them and perceive what appears to be injustice running rampant in the world around them.

"That's just not fair." "Well, she certainly didn't deserve that." "He was so young to be taken from us." "They work so hard, and they just can't seem to make any progress." "Divorce is so hard on the children." "What a bully."

These are comments we hear every day, along with too many others to count. Sometimes, our world seems to be so out of kilter that it seems balance will never return.

Our loved ones die, sometimes lingering, painful deaths. It is hard for us to understand how a 'just' God would allow this to happen. A child may suffer a losing battle with leukemia, or a host of other terrible childhood diseases.

Television plays a big part in our perception of the injustice that afflicts us worldwide. In an appeal for help, we see the havoc that results from the relentless ravages of starvation and disease in third world nations.

Maimed and dying or dead soldiers and civilians is common daily fare on television news reports. We see the outward destruction of buildings and homes. But what we do not see is the destruction of infrastructure, the destruction of hope. And we most certainly do not see the destruction of lives, the destruction of families. We fail to perceive the overwhelming loss of a promise for a future.

We see our politicians' endless debating over what appears to be either self-serving or generally meaningless topics, and are troubled that our leaders seem to have forgotten we are a nation founded by the people, of the people, and for the people. We persist in the hope that our nation is a haven for all of the people, all of the time. Always!

We see evidence everywhere that all is not well. We see battered women's shelters—and are glad they provide a safe haven. But wouldn't it be nice if women didn't need to be protected from the men they love? Wouldn't it be nice if the wives and children of these batterers weren't so compromised?

We see storage sheds for rent even in many small towns. We

have always been a nation on the move, and storage sheds, in that instance, serve a definite need. But many more storage sheds are in use because a marriage is broken, a home is broken, a family is broken.

Multitudes of homeless people wander the streets of our nation's cities each day, without purpose or hope. Many are veterans who have faithfully served their country, given all that they had to give, and yet they are homeless, most without any tangible help—no food, and no shelter. Many suffer from drug or alcohol addictions. Some suffer mental health problems. They live without dignity. In a nation rich beyond imagining in natural resources, goods and services, how can this be possible?

The list of 'things needing to be fixed' is endless.

America is predominantly a nation of Christians who believe that it is not only right, but incumbent upon them to help the less fortunate. Taken as a whole, this is not such a bad idea.

Most of us have been 'down on our luck' at one time or another. Most of us could site the turning point in our lives, where we were able to regroup and go forward once more in a positive manner. This often involved a single act of kindness, or a single point of inspiration.

Certainly, the fulfillment of 'acting as the Good Samaritan' results in help for others. Even more than that, though, it is a help to those who are dispensing whatever help is needed. Helping another, with an open heart, is a full circle communication, a full circle healing not for one soul, but two…or more.

The downside to accepting help is that 'strings' may often be attached. Some well-meaning people continue to believe and perpetuate the myth that a down-on-their-luck person must by virtue thereof be lazy, uneducated, or ignorant, as well. Those who embrace this template for native peoples worldwide believe it is their God-given duty to educate and to convert to Christianity these 'poor souls'—for their own good, of course.

Whether to fix or not to fix from a Native American standpoint is an extremely delicate matter.

Some aspects of 'fixing' are the direct result of ancient dictates, such as providing game for those in need—the elderly, those wounded or ill, and for families left without men to provide for them. So, some things can be changed.

Some things cannot be changed.

Some things should not be changed.

No aspect of an individual's right to choose his or her free will path must ever be violated. Even when you feel an individual is on a disastrous collision course, remember that it is his or her free will choice. You have no right to interfere. You have a sacred obligation not to interfere.

If you choose to interfere anyway, be aware that you are disrespecting Creator and the individual by not honoring the contract between them.

Naturally, when you see a person hanging by one hand from a cliff, you do your best to pull him to safety. Likewise, when a person is about to 'go down for the third time,' if you can save him from drowning, it is a good thing to try to save him.

The difference in stepping forward to help someone directly correlates to whether or not he can still help himself. That too, is a matter for deep contemplation, since many situations are not clearly delineated.

Practically speaking, if you do not save the man hanging from the cliff, or the drowning man, he will have no more opportunities to make free will decisions in this life, decisions that can define the spiritual nature of his walk on the Good Red Road.

"This is the worst thing that ever happened to me. I just don't know how I am going to be able to deal with it."

How often have we found ourselves mouthing those words? How often have we listened to a friend speak those words? More often than we would like. More often than we are comfortable with. More often than we think we can 'rise to the occasion.'

Our initial reaction might be one of complete shock and absolute panic. "What will I do? How will I live?" The shock reaction we experience often triggers an adrenalin reaction—the old fight or flight response. Sometimes we are left literally shaking from head to toe, but this feeling subsides fairly quickly as the adrenalin flow lessens, allowing us to think more clearly.

And how often do we later realize that "the worst thing that

241

ever happened to me" turned out to be "the best thing that ever happened to me!"

I believe before we were born, a sacred contract was agreed to between our Creator and us. I believe our lives are lived in pursuit of this sacred agreement as we do our best to follow The Good Red Road. I believe this contract is agreed to in such a way that it may be fulfilled in a host of different ways; in short, the way the contract is fulfilled is not carved in stone. It is a flexible contract, which may be changed by our use of free will at various points in the journey. Though our journey may appear to be circuitous, and often fraught with difficulties and complexities, it may still be attained—in this lifetime. I believe our great gift from Creator is this sacred pursuit, this ultimate opportunity to achieve our goal.

When questions arise concerning whether to fix or not to fix, do not think with your linear mind. Go to your heart, your center, and trust your instincts.

When I am in a quandary about what to do, I quiet my mind and listen patiently within the solitude. And I am often reminded by the Old Ones—"Don't Push the River."

The Cycle of Life

Spring, summer, autumn, winter, spring...this particular cycle of life appears not subject to change. We humans find the miracle of our annual planetary orbit around our sun reassuring, a veritable touchstone for regularity.

Earlier this spring, I chanced upon two young foxes rolling and playing like kittens, so absorbed at play that they were totally unaware of my presence. This occurred in a wooded, hilly, residential area, not far from a steep drop from a cliff. The little ones, however, seemed surefooted and sure of themselves as they raced back and forth along the edge of the ravine. Though rural, I was amazed to see the little foxes living in such close proximity to a populated area.

As the days of spring lengthened into summer, I kept watch from time to time on these small ones. They became strong and healthy, seemingly growing by 'leaps and bounds.' Then, after awhile, I didn't see them any more. I thought perhaps their mother had moved them elsewhere or was teaching them to hunt and be on their own.

Recently, however, I saw one of these small foxes in a wooded area near my home. His camouflage was so complete that I was able to see him only when he moved.

His mother was not in evidence, nor sadly, was his sibling. He appeared to be entirely alone—and I worried about how he was surviving. I also wondered what had happened to his mother and 'brother.'

The fox was now big enough to hunt small rodents, of which there seemed to be a dearth, but still, he didn't appear to be doing well. Had his mother been able to teach him to hunt and to live on his own before she had to leave him? I worried that he wasn't getting enough to eat. I observed that, though Fox was very thin, he seemed healthy. He was watchful and alert and exhibited short bursts of power, which translated into great speed. Mostly, he trotted a good bit, but also paced back and forth a lot.

I had seen the fox just before my dog, Maxi and I went for our morning walk. While on our walk, we became accidental witnesses to a killing. A squirrel scurrying across the road was killed by a passing car. How suddenly, how violently, the cycle of life had been interrupted.

The worst had occurred and another squirrel lay dead, killed by a sophisticated machine beyond his ability to comprehend as danger. The driver of the machine drove blissfully on, never knowing that a life had been destroyed in his passing, never knowing that one of Creator's blessings was now forever silenced.

Watching the 'killer car' speed away, I couldn't help but think how often we, ourselves, may serve as the casual destroyers of life?

How often do we hold ourselves accountable?

On our return from walking, Maxi and I paused again briefly before Squirrel. Respectfully, I offered prayers for a good journey for Squirrel. I asked Creator to allow Squirrel to live again in wholeness, health, happiness, and harmony with those of his or her own kind.

Once home, I hurried into the shower, intent on getting to an appointment on time. Preoccupied with thoughts of the appointment, I was surprised to hear one of the Old Ones say to me, "Get out of the shower."

"What?"

"Get out of the shower now!"

"What's going on? Am I going to be electrocuted or something?"

Mentally, I perceived what could only be the equivalent of a derisive snort from the Old Ones. I could visually see them shaking their heads in dismay at my inability to understand what was needed.

Patiently, the Old Ones explained, "Go to Squirrel and ask his spirit for permission to give of his body that Fox may live."

Of course! Why didn't I think of that?

And so it happened that I rushed forth from the shower and, still dripping, managed to get into my clothes, run a comb through my hair, and hurried out the door. This was as good as my appearance was going to get for my appointment. There was something important that needed doing first. The appointment, for all practical purposes, did not matter. What was about to transpire next was truly a matter of life and death.

Tears were coursing down my face as I looked with sorrow upon this small broken creature, only moments away from being so sassy, and so alive. Squirrel lay serene, gently cradled in the embrace of the shovel, his tail ruffling gently in the light breeze like a triumphant banner, celebrating the renewal of spirit, and the cycle of life on-going.

As I carefully bore Squirrel to his new destination, I thought of how alive, how bright with intensity and alertness he had been —just moments before. "There is a lesson here for all of us," I thought.

Carefully, I placed Squirrel in a quiet place where Fox was sure to find him. I thought again of the perfect beauty of the cycle of life.

And the words came to me: for everything there is a time, for everything there is a season...

The Road Ahead

I was on vacation, visiting my family in Colorado. My sister and I were out driving one beautiful morning. We had been climbing so gradually, I was almost unaware that we were steadily gaining altitude.

Suddenly, we topped a rise. I felt a sudden intake of breath as I literally gasped at the sheer magnificence of the view before us. This two-lane narrow ribbon of a road we found ourselves on undulated gradually downward in ever decreasing, surreal splendor, as far as the eye could see. Finally, the road disappeared altogether, still reaching toward the mountains, which both dwarfed us and, yet, appeared so distant.

This got me to thinking about perceptions.

I began to think about the impact being a mixed-blood Native American has had upon my life—and the lives of other mixed-blood Native American people known to me. On the surface, our life experiences and perceptions have many common denominators, as well as many differences.

Much is said about walking our talk. It is important for us to act responsibly, to walk in a good way, to set a good example for the young ones.

Most of us were not born on a reservation. Most of us have not grown up on a reservation. Most of us have not been schooled on a reservation. Like many of our full-blood counterparts, we have not had the opportunity to learn to speak in our native tongue, nor did we have the opportunity to learn the traditions and ceremonies of old. In these and many other ways, therefore, our paths have been intensely individual, so that the seeking of our true paths became a vastly different personal truth for each of us.

We have lived in the White world a long time now. However it came to pass, our ancestors intermingled with whites, thus creating a mix of bloods, cultures, and traditions, heretofore unknown. For all practical purposes, we are an entirely new breed of people.

While our uniqueness is accepted with varying degrees of pride among us, our Good Red Road is not always an easy path to follow. Our duality is often confusing and frequently discouraging. We feel we do not belong in either the 'White' world or the 'Red' world. Many of us feel adrift and powerless to control the course of our lives.

How do we best walk in a good way? Do we follow the old ways, as we are able to understand them? Do we remain true to traditional native values and ways of life, adhering to the spiritual ways of our ancestors? Or do we embrace our White culture? Do we embrace Christianity, with all that Christianity implies? Or do we find our way to a 'middle' road, previously un-trod and, for all practical purposes, untested.

Speaking for myself alone, I listen closely to the Old Ones, who have, without interfering with my free will, guided and directed me as I have traveled The Good Red Road. The Old Ones have been, and continue to be, my teachers, my advisors, and my protectors. It is impossible for me to imagine the spiritual poverty I might have experienced without The Old Ones helping to create the harmony and balance that is at the core center of my life, my being.

I believe that each person, each animal, each tree, each rock, each insect, and all their ancestors for all time—for that matter, the whole of the natural world—has left a mark, like an invisible footprint or personal energy print as it lives and passes. I believe that all living things sing a song of life. It is an experience without parallel to be still enough within self to listen to, and to truly hear, the songs of rocks, trees, and 'others.'

I have spent a lifetime reading signs to help me understand and determine my direction. I have always been able to 'read between the lines' where men and women are concerned. I hear what is not said. I see what is not visible. And that, too, helps me to know the truth of others, and whether interaction with others is to be desired or avoided.

We learn from negative, as well as positive, reinforcement. Since thoughts are so very powerful, I feel it is incumbent upon us to dwell on the negative as little as possible. While it is important to recognize the role of negativity in the balance of power, I choose to think in a positive way. I believe if enough people choose to think in a positive way, we can change the world—for the better!

So we have this life, an amazing, ongoing opportunity for growth, where we learn to love and be loved, and to honor and appreciate the magnitude of all living things.

Where does the road ahead lead? Each of us must answer that for ourselves.

The road ahead beckons to me, calls to me, challenges me to follow, beguiling me with a graceful flow toward the splendid, ethereal, far-away mountains.

And then, too ...I hear the road singing.

Mid-Course Correction

The time had come for the Shaman and me to part ways. We had known from the beginning of our journey together that this must happen, but knowing and experiencing are two very different venues.

We had been brought together at the behest of the Old Ones. I was taught by the Grandmothers how to heal the Shaman. Then, too, the Shaman told me I would be helping him when he served as the hollow bones in the healing of others. These two 'callings' alone might have absorbed a lifetime. But there was much more to our relationship than that, and we served as both teacher and student, one to the other.

For three years, our lives had been so intertwined that it was sometimes hard to tell where one person left off and the other began. When the Shaman held my hands in his, the physical sense of touch was replaced with the spiritual energy of touch. Each of us ceased to feel the physical hands, and felt only spiritual energy. There is no real way to explain such a profound experience. If you have not experienced shared mutual energy, there is no way it can truly be explained. Needless to say, after being such an integral part of one another for the better part of three years, shock and profound feelings of loss were the hallmarks of our departure, one from the other. A great many tears were shed by each of us in the process as we physically stepped away from one another to take up our new lives.

Though my home, my job, my family, my friends, and my loving canine companion—the outward 'trappings' of my life—had not changed, and were of considerable comfort, my personal reality had changed significantly. I felt as though I had been abruptly thrown into an entirely new dimension, and had been found wanting.

As I worked my way through feelings of loss and abandonment, grieving for what I perceived to be lost, slowly I began to establish a renewed sense of unity and harmony within myself. And with restored harmony came the realization that no one who ever impacts our life is lost to us. We go forward carrying the loving memory of that person within us and, by so doing, continue to be an ongoing part of one another. To this day, I feel no "real" separation from the Shaman. If anything, the physical separation from the Shaman seemed to bring about new insights, new understanding, and newfound confidence. Ideas, dreams and visions now filled my days and nights. I was immersed in a 'sea' without horizons; knowledge was flooding in and out of my consciousness like a vibrant tide. I was hard pressed to remember —and aware that it was not necessary for me to remember—that all I was learning was stored in my subconscious, complete with trigger mechanisms that would bring the information forth when it was the right time for it to be released.

Time seemed to be speeding up! It was progressing at a full gallop. That was my observation. Days seemed to melt into other days, weeks into months, with no line of demarcation whatsoever. Whole weeks just seemed to disappear in the expanding blur of my newfound perception of reality.

Occasionally, I wondered if I were losing my tenuous grip on reality entirely, but, most days, I dismissed this thought with the self-reassurance that if I were really 'that far gone,' chances are that I wouldn't be aware enough to wonder about it.

I began to have even more dreams and visions than usual. What was I experiencing? I couldn't be sure. Ideas swirled through my mind as numerous as leaves falling from the trees in autumn, blowing along the ground, the myriad shapes and sizes coming to rest briefly in heaps of red, yellow, green, coral, and rust before once again taking to the air in search of their individual unknown destinations.

So it was with my mind as the dreams and visions continued to flow into my 'ordinary' consciousness. How had I come to this point in time, this fork in the road? Which branch of the road should I take? One thing I knew for certain. The path I chose was critical to my ability to accomplish my life goals. Without hesitation, I chose the way of The Good Red Road, and was only a little surprised to see the "Y" branches of the road come together, blending clearly and strongly into a single center road.

Of course! Once again, The Old Ones had provided me with an unmistakable sign. I couldn't help but smile as I set my feet upon this newfound path. As I began walking, I found myself humming a little song, a song of happiness.

New Life Paths for Everyone

I thought about how The Old Ones help us to find our true path, how they work to continue to keep us on The Good Red Road. I had spent the past thirty years in the South, and had never considered living again in the American heartland. But here I was, living not fifty miles from where I was born and had gone to school. And it was the doing of The Old Ones, helping me to fulfill my unremembered contract with Creator.

Mother had been diagnosed with cancer, and had part of one lung removed. After treatment, she seemed to be recovering nicely; her prognosis was encouraging. Since Mother appeared to be doing fine, I decided to work until I could spend a couple of vacation weeks with her. In the meantime, I spoke with Mom on the phone several times a day. In speaking to her on the phone, I had no idea her Alzheimer's had progressed to such an aggressive level.

I was shocked when a friend of Mom's, who was a nurse, called to alert me that she no longer felt it was safe for Mother to live alone. And I was even more shocked when a male relative, and a neighbor, called me independently of one another to give me the same message.

I was beyond distraught. I immediately spoke with my employer. It was agreed that I would be allowed an indefinite leave of absence from my job, without pay, so that I might visit with Mother and assess the situation first-hand.

Early one morning, with my companion, Maxi, and a single suitcase, I left to drive north for an extended visit with Mother.

As I pulled out of the driveway that day, I could not foresee that I would never again return to my balmy, active, 'southern' life, never again live in the house my husband and I had made into a home, a place of loving warmth and hospitality. Our southern home was truly a place that radiated happiness.

Instead, as I took to the open road that breezy early November day, my life was like an open book; I had no idea what to expect and I was making no assumptions. Without hesitation or design, I was simply turning the page to my next life chapter. With each passing mile, my 'old life' receded more and more into a past of fond memories.

Unfortunately, what Mother's friends had told me was indeed true; her Alzheimer's disease had worsened considerably and it was probably more apparent to me than those who visited with her every day. How had I not been able to recognize the signs? I realized that most of our conversations had taken place in the mornings when Mother was at her best. In retrospect, I realized that Mom had allowed me to do most of the talking. At any rate, I was not prepared for Mother's extreme mood swings, alternating from passive behavior to sudden bouts of anger.

Mother had always been an independent woman. She was proud, intelligent, charming, and persuasive. She could also be tough, pragmatic, and resilient. Mom could quickly assess any situation, and easily respond to difficulty with originality and finesse. My brother, sister, and I always looked up to our father and mother. Had they not been our parents, we agreed, we would still have loved them, and certainly would have honored and respected them.

Suddenly, however, without our knowledge or consent, Mother was the child, and I found myself thrust into the role of the mother. On some unconscious, indescribable level, we both adjusted to that situation, and it was with wry humor that I often found myself making decisions and responding accordingly by thinking, "How would Mom handle this situation?"

Mother, now, was my all-consuming passion. I will always be grateful to my employer for insisting that I leave immediately to spend time with Mom, for it was in those first six weeks that Mother was 'more herself.' It was during that time that Mom and I were able to go out on short shopping expeditions, able to enjoy riding out in the car to visit a friend, or go out to dinner. During that time, Mother and I even planned and implemented hosting a surprise fiftieth wedding celebration for close family friends.

Mother's home had always served as an impromptu 'open house,' a meeting place where the coffeepot was always full and everyone was welcome, day or night. For years, one of Mom's lady friends, and a cousin who was more like an older brother, met most mornings for coffee and conversation.

The centerpiece for Mom's ongoing 'open house' was her big rectangular kitchen table, made of wood, and centered in the main part of her light, airy, old-fashioned kitchen. A serving cart against one wall was perpetually stocked with a full coffee pot, a variety of cups and spoons, as well as cream and sugar.

This area served as a 'round' table for discussions on history, world events, local gossip, and things in general. 'Hot' topics of interest were discussed, pro and con, with considerable vigor. We teased Mom about acting as the 'Devil's Advocate,' but our label was not well received, and we quickly ceased to use it.

In truth, Mother had such a sense of fair play that if any idea or person were 'under attack' without representation, she felt compelled to defend the position of that person or idea, even though it might not represent her own personal belief. It could be said in all fairness that Mother was a life-long advocate of the 'underdog.' She left no stone unturned in defending those who were not present to defend themselves.

My fondest memory about those morning get-togethers and the ongoing coffee klatches in Mother's kitchen is how often the room seemed to be rocked by laughter.

Being back at Mom's, I had the opportunity to spend time with a Native American childhood friend. We had been in touch over the years from time to time, and had recently begun to attend Pow Wows together. I was able to visit with this friend every time I came back to Mother's, as she lived nearby. She had introduced me to other native people, who comprised a diverse group, made up of mostly mixed-blood people. Since the people represented many different tribes, understandably, customs and traditions were often different. Nevertheless, common ground was established so that it provided a 'comfort' zone for everyone. We had become a close, but loose-knit, community.

In a kind of a gauzy dream, the days flowed quickly past and my sister soon arrived from Colorado to spend the Thanksgiving holiday with us.

Over many cups of coffee, we talked about everything. All of us were excited that our Brother was coming back to spend Christmas with Mom and me. Rightly, my sister was making Christmas at home for her children. Nevertheless, we wished it might have been possible for my sister, her children, and our brother to visit Mother and me, so that all of us could have been there at the same time. Mother said, "Well, we're *always* together in spirit." Her message was not lost on my sister and me.

Sometimes, just the three of us, Mother, my sister, and I sat together talking quietly, loving one another through cherished memories. By day, we sometimes took a drive to places where Mom had grown up, and to places where we had all once lived.

Thanksgiving Day morning, Mom's dear lady friend, who resided in a nursing home, was brought by her daughter for a visit. Once again, the three friends, Mother, her lady friend, and her brother-cousin met for coffee. It was a bittersweet meeting, with both the ladies suffering ill health. Sadly, it was the last time the three friends were to be together in this life.

Who could have predicted that sunny, happy, Thanksgiving Day that just three months later, these three dear friends would have departed from this Earth?

Mother was the first to go, and just ten days later, the other two friends crossed and were buried within a few days of one another.

With a sad heart, I arrived at my mother's brother-cousin's visitation. I was comforted to see his son, my cousin, standing with our other cousin. Along with my younger brother, we three cousins, all the same age, had grown up together, almost as a single family.

Distraught and tearful, seeking to ease my cousin's painful loss, I said, "I know what's going on here."

His look was questioning.

"Somewhere in Heaven," I said, "there's a new coffee klatch going on." We three cousins, always so close, smiled, and for that moment in time, we felt a little better.

The Regalia Chronicles

I had a dream, a dream sent by the Grandmothers. Their message to me was clear—it was now time for me to dance—at Pow Wows. I thrilled to the dance, always acutely aware of the connection evidenced by the dancers—as the visual heartbeat of the drum. The drum acts as a physical reminder of the heartbeat of Mother Earth. To dance to the beat of the drum is to dance in rhythm with the Mother. It is a way of reconnecting to spirit through harmony. And now, I had been called to the dance. The thought was overwhelming to me. This would not simply be the act of joining the other dancers in the arena. I knew that the dance had to be performed in an exact way, rightly honoring tradition and all of those who had gone before. This was not an honor to be undertaken lightly. In a very real sense, the dance was an ongoing prayer of thanksgiving to our Creator.

I explained to some of my Native friends that I had been called to the dance, and asked if they would help me to learn. They were both gracious and patient in their teaching, and as I continued to practice the dance, I began to 'hear' the beat of the drum. I relaxed into the dance, feeling not only comfortable, but also joyful as I danced.

The more I danced, the more the voice of the Grandfather—Thunderbird Dancer—sang in my ears. "The words are in the Dance," he often recounted. "The words are in the Dance." 'The words' I took to refer to prayer and to life itself, our joyful, ongoing connection with Creator. As an elder, the form of 'my' dance was expected to embody the spirit of serenity and dignity. While being very comfortable with this form of dance, my spirit soared as I danced, much as though I were doing a more active form of dance—such as the butterfly dance. I was happy dancing. I felt I had 'come home' to the dance.

I needed to wear regalia to dance in the sacred circle in the arena at Pow Wows—and I had none. Once again, my native friends came to the rescue. One of my friends, Redwing Blackbird, was a seamstress, and she graciously agreed to sew my dress.

My dress had to be very simple, that much I had been shown. My Celtic friend, Erin and I found the perfect material for the dress —faun-colored faux suede. The material was softly elegant and fell, naturally and with grace, to the ankles. At a glance, the suede cloth looked exactly like leather.

My friend Redwing was excited about making the dress, and began sewing almost immediately. She used a Southern Plains cloth pattern, using one of her own dresses for a template, and she had no trouble cutting out the material for the dress.

However, when Redwing began to sew the dress on her machine, all kinds of problems cropped up. She tried again and again to sew the dress, but to no avail. Finally, exasperated, my friend put the dress aside for a little while to consider this difficulty. Was the material too 'slippery?' No, she had sewn similar materials many times before on her machine with no problem.

As Redwing considered the situation, she later told me, the Old Ones indicated to her that the dress was to be made entirely by hand, that not a single stitch was to be made by a machine. The dress was to be made in the old way.

Always ready for a new challenge, my friend began again to sew the dress—this time, stitch by stitch, and as Redwing sewed, she began to experience a host of sensations and insights. The dress making time passed as though it were a dream, she said, and, before long, it was finished.

As the project neared completion, Redwing asked what kind of ornamentation I would like on the dress, offering several attractive suggestions. Though I agreed that ornamentation would be very nice, somehow it just didn't seem right for this particular dress. This I told her, reiterating that the dress was to be very plain.

Following our conversation, in another dream I saw myself wearing this beautiful dress with my knee-high suede leather moccasins, and on the left sleeve of the dress was a red hand, a red hand that looked as if it had been dipped in blood and pressed to the sleeve! Strongly imprinted, the fingers stretched wide, the thumb reached at almost a right angle to the left, or towards my heart, the separated fingers stretched strongly upward into a loose embrace of the upper arm.

This brought forward yet another step in the process. Life, the Old Ones continue to remind me, and all that it entails, is always a process. Learning is always a process. Our true path is always a process. And so, too, was the making of my regalia—a process.

What was the significance of this red hand? The red hand, the Old Ones explained, was an ancient symbol representative of the blood of the people, all that the people stand for, the power and history of the people, and it would be placed on the left sleeve for two reasons. The left side of my body, they explained, was my spiritual side. The other reason was because, as I danced clockwise within the sacred circle, the red hand would clearly be visible by those outside the arena and would carry a message to everyone who saw the symbol.

How was this red hand to be placed on the dress? My Celtic friend, Erin, and I are very connected, and she has a great affinity for the Indian people. It was she who had the definitive dream that opened up the next 'chapter' in the regalia chronicles.

Erin's dream went a step further than my dream. In her dream, not only did she see the red hand on the dress sleeve, but she also saw a holy man conducting the ceremony. Who this person was, Erin had no idea, but she said he was a person of stature, a descendant of a powerful, well-known Native American family.

Once more, another step in the process was approached. I asked Redwing if she knew anyone who 'fit the description,' anyone who could do the ceremony. She laughed, instantly recognizing who this person was. Redwing introduced him to Erin and me, and I respectfully requested that he conduct the ceremony. He agreed on the condition that we first undergo purification in a sweat lodge. We readily agreed. Another first!

Erin and I were shocked to learn that the man who had agreed to do the ceremony was the great-grandson of a holy man so famous that even now, many years after his death, his was a name with which we were instantly familiar. I was 'blown away' that he would consider doing the ceremony. Redwing smiled at us indulgently; he was her friend.

Once again, Redwing proved to be an invaluable source of guidance about sweat lodge protocol. She made us aware of proper dress and behavior before, during, and after the sweat. It was proper to give thanks with a gift of importance for such a ceremony.

It did not take me long to deliberate on what to get; I had seen a beautiful blanket, with a Sioux Star in the very center of the blanket. The blanket was rich with a mixture of red, black, and blue, as well as other highlighted colors. I thought it the most beautiful blanket I had ever seen. My friends agreed it was the perfect gift for saying 'thank you.'

At last, the day of the red hand ceremony arrived.

Excitement and anticipation were in the air. My friends, Redwing, Erin, and I were going to take part in a sweat lodge! We arrived half an hour before the ceremony to be greeted warmly by the facilitator, our hostess, and the other participants. We were acquainted with everyone gathered, except two, who made us feel welcome, as well.

A huge fire was burning and I couldn't help but think that the way the wood was laid within, it looked like a miniature teepee. I noticed almost at once the red hot rocks heating in the ashes.

Before the fire pit on an 'Indian' blanket rested a buffalo skull so filled with white sage that it protruded from the eye sockets. The skull itself was beautifully painted and, as I stood before this Native shrine, a feeling of deep melancholy briefly touched me, quickly followed by a great sense of belonging, of a connection that far surpassed the moment, the place, and the time.

I was overcome by powerful feelings struggling to the surface of my consciousness. My anxiety disappeared in an instant, as I felt empowered with an overall sense of serenity and rightness.

Once the purifying sweat had taken place, once the red hand ceremony had been completed, I knew, without doubt, that the life I had known was over. My life would now be divided into all that had gone before this ceremony and all that would occur following the red hand ceremony.

With a feeling of great reverence, Erin and I placed our gifts of tobacco and sage on the blanket near the buffalo skull. We carefully placed the regalia to be blessed in ceremony on the blanket, along with the 'thank you' blanket wrapped in red flannel and tied with red ribbon, a feather, and some sage.

I was overcome with emotion. Tears began to flow in silent rivulets down my cheeks, and Redwing came quietly to my side and put her arm around me. Seeing my tears, the facilitator nodded, his gentle smile reassuring me.

"Why don't you change your clothes in the house, now?" he suggested. "We'll begin soon."

Making a hurried trip back to our car, my friend and I carried food we had prepared for the feast to follow the sweat and the ceremony into our hostess' home. We also carried with us our 'sweat lodge clothes.' We quickly changed into floor length cotton dresses with sleeves that came to our elbows. We carried with us towels to take into the lodge.

The facilitator was waiting for us. He directed us to remove our shoes and, as we stood barefoot, shivering slightly in the November chill, one by one, he purified us with sage before we entered the lodge.

The construction of the sweat lodge was round and low to the ground, and the facilitator told us how to enter, asking me to enter first, since the ceremony about to begin would require me to be seated next to him. Without speaking, we kneeled and quietly crawled into the sweat lodge to our assigned places. I sat up carefully, my head nearly touching one of the willow saplings that formed the dome of the lodge. Sitting cross-legged, we found ourselves crowded into a close circle around the 'fire pit.' Including the facilitator, we numbered seven—a number I have always considered sacred.

Emotions were running rampant as we were seated inside the lodge. The facilitator would enter the lodge last; he would be seated to my left, closest to the door. The other participants sat to my right. Just before the facilitator entered, I saw beyond the open door myriads of sparks from the fire, shooting into the night sky like so many Roman candles. For just a moment, they burned brightly before settling to Earth. Once more, the sky became brilliant with the light of stars without number. I heard a sharp intake of breath, and realized, with a small sense of detachment, that it came from me.

Just before the door to the lodge closed, I noticed the shadowy figure of the fire keeper silhouetted by the light cast by the fire. The first of the heated stones—the 'grandfathers'—to be used in the sweat were gathered at the edge of the fire, so that they could be brought quickly and easily into the lodge at the appropriate time.

The facilitator entered the lodge and seated himself. The heated rocks were brought into the lodge, and welcomed by the participants. Bits of sage, sweet grass, and cedar were dropped onto them, throwing off welcome, comforting, familiar scents.

Once the grandfathers were in place, a bucket of water with a dipper was brought into the lodge, and placed beside the facilitator.

Abruptly, he closed the door and we were immersed at once into a darkness that was so absolute as to constitute complete darkness.

I had never been in a lodge before and was overwhelmed by the sensations I was feeling. With no preconceived ideas as to what was about to happen, I listened carefully as the facilitator began gently to guide us through the steps of the opening ceremony into the time honored, ongoing personal journey of spirituality and insight provided by the sweat lodge.

My mind seemed to be almost a thing apart from me, operating at once on separate frequencies, allowing me to think about and experience many things at once. As I took part in the pipe ceremony, listening to the prayers, the singing, the drumming, the chanting and others speaking, I thought I had never been so alive, never so aware, never so finely attuned to the universe and all within it.

I felt I had known the other participants throughout the annals of time. There was no difference in us. We were made of the same stuff; we had come from the stars, and we were here together now as one, and would forever go on as one entity, one great cosmic, spiritual vessel filled with the fluidity of reason and knowledge, compassion and understanding, truth beyond anything we could imagine, and yet we were able to imagine. Imagine...

I keenly felt the spirits of the Native grandfathers and grandmothers who had sat in countless sweat lodges throughout time, where those seeking insight and knowledge were reassured and healed, resonating to their visions. I felt as one with them, could feel their presence and their support for the path of personal truth I found myself on.

Time in the lodge was time without beginning or end. Time was both accelerated and brought to a complete halt. I found myself adrift in a particular time and space I had never before experienced, and yet it felt perfect, complete. The lodge was filled to bursting with the good spirits of the ancestors, our love and honor for them.

The steaming heat of the lodge, while intense, was bearable— just bearable. The air seemed almost too hot to breathe. From time to time, it was all I could do to remain conscious. My breathing was shallow, my pulse erratic, and I felt as though I could 'go out like a light' at any moment. Occasionally, I felt extremely nauseated. I steadfastly pushed these thoughts and feelings away, seeking escape from physical discomfort by moving deeper and with greater awareness into the visions I was experiencing.

I became aware that the facilitator was praying in Lakota. Following the prayer, there was silence. He opened the door to let in fresh air, as he had done several times before during the lodge. "Good sweat," he said, nodding. Good sweat."

The facilitator asked us to come out of the lodge while he made preparations for the Red Hand Ceremony. One by one, we crawled from the lodge and were slowly helped to our feet by the facilitator and the fire-keeper. I was surprised to find myself feeling light-headed and weak.

We were advised to drink some water, but very slowly, so as not to become ill. We gathered near the fire to keep warm until the ceremony. I suddenly realized that I was 'wringing wet' with sweat, my dress soaked, my hair wet, and that, indeed, I was chilled. Surprisingly, my bare feet were not cold at all.

Emerging from the moist heat of the lodge into the crisp and chilly starlit November night, while a bit of a shock was really quite bracing. Before long, my feelings of weakness and light-headedness passed and, as I stood by the fire, I gradually began to warm up. My breathing became more 'normal.'

I felt hollow, 'light as a feather.' Feelings of intensity and awareness surged through my entire being as I stood bemused, grinning at the fire as though I were responding to some internal joke I had just heard.

So, I thought, the sweat is over! I was shocked to learn that hours had passed. It seemed as though we had entered the sweat only moments before, and now it was over.

My silent musing was interrupted by overwhelming feelings of loss and separation, suddenly consuming me with deep sadness. Briefly, I longed for the powerful connection to Spirit so recently experienced.

As the facilitator and Erin were mixing the red paint that was to simulate the blood of the people to be placed on my left sleeve, the facilitator told me to go into the house, towel off, put on my regalia dress, and return as quickly as possible.

In just a few minutes, I was back with the others at the fire. I checked with Redwing to make sure I had the dress on 'right side to,' expressing concern that the red hand be placed correctly on the left sleeve, as seen in the vision.

Once more, we were all gathered in the lodge—this time for the Red Hand Ceremony. It was a beautiful ceremony. And all the while, I was extremely conscious of the Old Ones smiling, blessing us all with their loving presence.

Once again, time seemed to stretch and bend to span what seemed to be an all-too-brief space of time for such an important event. In reality, another half hour had passed. The ceremony was completed and we found ourselves, once again, standing beside the blazing fire.

I felt exhilarated. I felt proud, not for myself, but proud that I heard the Old Ones when they spoke, proud of my friends, who had their own visions and insights concerning the Red Hand, and thankful to them for helping bring this ceremony to fruition.

I felt proud of the facilitator. Every fiber of my being recognized and felt the intrinsic rightness, the sacredness, of the way he had conducted the Red Hand Ceremony. Yes, I was proud that the facilitator had been the one to perform this amazing ceremony, proud that he served as the guiding light in honoring the wishes of the Old Ones.

I presented the facilitator with the Sioux Star blanket, and he gave me a gift, as well." He wrapped himself immediately in the blanket. It was clear to see he treasured it. I thanked the Old Ones for guiding me to the perfect gift to honor this ceremony.

Once again, all participants changed back to casual clothes—jeans and warm shirts and jackets. Then we gathered in the house for a very welcome feast. We were all thirsty and hungry, but were so excited, at first, that we could barely eat.

Food had rarely tasted so good to me. I ate voraciously, but slowly, savoring each bite, enjoying the flavor and seasoning as if for the first time.

Energy poured forth from each one of us, drenching the room in conversation and feelings that galvanized us all to a more enervated, excited state. Once again, I felt as though I had never been so alive.

Now, where had I experienced this feeling before? I felt so sharply 'in tune,' each of my senses so acute, that the feeling stopped just short of physical pain.

Gradually, the friendly, animated conversation in the warm kitchen gave way to a sort of comforting background buzzing. And suddenly, I remembered.

I was a child. I had awakened to find myself in a very cold room, heavy covers piled over my small body. The covers were so heavy that I couldn't move. I called out for my mother. She came immediately into the room, smiling. "So, you're awake at last," she said. "You had a really high fever, but it's almost back to normal now. Are you hungry?"

I nodded. "Yes, I think so. And I'm really thirsty."

"Okay, then," she replied. "I'll be right back."

As I waited for Mother's return, I realized for the first time in days, I could breathe through my nose. I began to focus on my breathing, first holding my breath, then exhaling noisily. I sighted down my nose, first with one eye, then the other. I discovered, as if for the first time, that I could close one nostril simply by holding a finger against the outside of my nose. This I explored on both sides. The intake and outgo of air through my nasal passages was so sharp, so acutely 'clear,' that it almost hurt.

Where was Mom with the food? I suddenly felt ravenous.

And what was that 'flashing?' I watched, with delight, a small shaft of sunlight, animated by a slight draft, dancing lazily across the top blanket on my bed. This light show was so sharply clear to my eyes that I squinted against the glare. I felt renewed just to see it and, looking up at the broken place in the wall where it shone through, I smiled. Aha! I had located the source. I lay back, breathing easily, waiting for breakfast. I felt so warm, so cozy, and *so* sleepy. I dozed.

"Margo!" Mom was calling me. "Margo."

"I'll be right there, Mom."

Abruptly, I was jolted back to the present by the laughter of my friends.

"Where are you?" someone chided.

"We're over here." another chimed in.

"No, over here," a friend laughed.

I grinned sheepishly. "Sorry," I said. "I didn't mean to be rude."

I looked about me at the beautiful home my friends and I had been invited to enjoy. Looking at the abundance and variety of food, and the sheer opulence of it all, I couldn't help but smile once more. The contrast from present time to my childhood was like night and day.

"But, in the poverty of my childhood," I thought, "great riches were to be found."

I will always be grateful for my childhood. I learned to be independent, and yet dependent as a part of a greater whole. My siblings and I understood resilience and the power of keeping a good thought. We understood the power generated by true friendship. We understood the power of family. We understood the power of us!

What you believe is possible—*is* possible! Poverty, in my estimation, is a great tool in learning to live into your personal truth at an early age—and to recognize and embrace the endless possibilities presented as a result.

"Are you ready to head for the barn?" Erin asked.

"Ready," I answered, grinning.

We gathered up the containers we had brought food in, thanked our hostess and the facilitator, hugged them and the other participants, and were on our way.

It was near midnight when my friend, who was driving, and I started for home. The night was crisp and dark. The barest sliver of a new moon stood out in the sky and the stars stood out like beacons. The sky seemed so close that we felt we could almost reach up and touch it.

It was about an hour's drive to reach home, but it seemed only minutes before we found ourselves pulling into Erin's driveway. Once in her vehicle, we couldn't wait to share our feelings and thoughts about what we had experienced. We talked the entire duration of the drive.

Erin and I were acutely aware that the ceremonies we had just taken part in marked the beginning for each of us, both separately and together, of a whole new dimension of our journey on the Good Red Road.

As I drove home from my friend's place, I heard The Old Ones say, "Remember, everything is a process. Remember."

Mile Marker 111—Live Into Your Dreams

I don't claim to know much about dreams—I only know what I know. I have done no study on the subject, but, like Native Americans since the beginning of time, I discuss with others their dreams and mine, seeking to discover the true nature of a particular dream.

I believe before we come to this plane of existence, we plan not just one future for ourselves, but as many as half a dozen, several at the least. In these possible futures lie a number of entry points and exit points, all of which may radically alter the course of our lives, obviously.

I believe we work from an instinct of remembered outcomes. I believe our free will is uppermost in the shaping and ultimate destiny of our lives.

And I believe some of our dreams are to let us know we are on the right road; in short, mile marker 111.

Personally, I have had dreams of this nature all of my life. Often, I remembered the dream long enough to wonder at its meaning, forgot the dream, and then the dream came true—in every detail, at the proper time. I have been married three times, and two of the three husbands I dreamed about beforehand; yet, when I first met them, I did not recognize immediately who they were—and the importance in my life they were to represent.

I recognized each of the husbands only when they spoke the specific words of my dreams in the exact settings in my dreams. It was like a trigger mechanism to reassure me I was, indeed, following the right path.

Lots of our dreams I think of as expiation dreams, ridding us of excess baggage—pain, anxiety, depression, negativity of all sorts, etc.—so as to lighten our spiritual load.

Some dreams are to be experienced, for whatever reason. I dreamed of the Mount Saint Helen's volcanic eruption just hours before it happened. I didn't truly understand what I was seeing, however, until I woke up and watched the news on television.

In my dream, I was aware of a huge blast taking place, a tremendous explosion. I felt the concussion and watched, as though looking down from a great height, as thousands of trees were instantly incinerated. Beyond that, I watched, though still not understanding what I was seeing, miles and miles of trees laying down in a pattern, all facing downhill, all laid out in the same way in the same direction. Only later did I realize that this was the result of the concussion wave caused by the eruption.

In my dream, I saw places where people had died. I did not see the people, but there was some sort of a messaging imprint from them. One man in particular, I remember, was instantly aware of what had occurred. He heard the explosion just before the concussion hit him, killing him instantly. He experienced in that single instant no fear; instead, the feeling I got from him was a sense of awe—and disbelief.

Later, as I watched dogs searching for these people, each time a dog came to the site of someone's passing, I experienced a fleeting, but terrible, sense of sadness, of loss that was so primitive in its nature as to be nearly indescribable. I felt like sinking to my knees and howling in my grief. I felt like wailing to the heavens, rocking back and forth, so intense were the emotions I experienced. As I withdrew from the scene, I saw myself receding into the distance, still keening, rocking to and fro. I knew that this posture, the keening, the rocking, would carry through the night.

Since that time, I have rarely watched the news. Really important news will get through one way or another anyway. One of my friends chided me for choosing to be uninformed, and insisted on an explanation as to why I seldom watch the news.

"It just never seems to cheer me up," was my reply.

Step Away From the Trees

Knowledge is learning that 'has built upon itself' through trial and error, through personal experiences of success and failure. Knowledge is also observation—the quiet study of others, of self, of nature, and all things natural and man-made. Knowledge is about understanding how things work and, more importantly, how things *can* work; most important, however, is how things *should* work.

Knowledge calls into play introspection and self-criticism. Knowledge calls into play all of our ancient, as well as modern, techniques for survival itself. The built-in trigger mechanisms for survival of the species have not been washed away before the encroaching tide of a hyper-modern, technical world, with all its trappings.

Instead, these universal and time-tested 'allowances' for peace-making, for withdrawal from combat before one of us destroys another, and thus the balance of all things, have resurfaced in our lives, coming strongly into play when the need is greatest.

It is imperative, now more than at any other time in history, that we create the tools for learning to understand our neighbors— on a worldwide basis. Never before in history has the understanding of such relationships been of such critical importance.

How do we begin to reach out, to truly begin to 'walk in another man's moccasins?' The understanding we seek must begin with perception—and perspective. Like the man says, "it all depends on where you're standing."

When my brother and I were growing up, our comments on life often tried the patience of our mother beyond limits. I have to smile, thinking back to one particular occasion as, exasperated, Mother quoted the old saying, "You're too close to the forest to see the trees!"

As we began to open our mouths in protest, Mother silenced us by raising her hand with the palm upraised, 'pushing' the space between us as though to 'keep us at bay.'

As we once more opened our mouths to protest, she made a sort of abrupt hissing sound between her teeth as though to say, "Stop!"

Though she politely asked us to sit, we understood it was not a request. We took chairs at the kitchen table and, seated side by side, we faced our mother. "Only one of you may talk at a time," she advised. "We're going to discuss this."

As one, we nodded. "How do you know when you're in a forest?" Mom asked.

"Easy," my brother replied, "You're surrounded by lots of trees." He grinned engagingly, sure that he had come up with the right answer.

"But how do you know *for sure* that you're in a forest," Mother pressed. "For all you know, you might just be in a grove of trees, or a small copse of trees, and not a forest at all."

"Well, you could walk for awhile," I chimed in, "and see how far the trees 'went.'"

"You could do that, certainly," Mother allowed, "but you might be going in circles, or you might be lost. You might be looking at the same trees time and again, and erroneously think you were in a huge forest."

We kids looked at one another uncomfortably, chagrined. "So, how *do* you tell the forest from the trees?" I finally asked in a small voice.

"Well, there are various ways," Mother explained. "You could climb one of the bigger trees to the top and look all around to see how far the trees extended."

"Oh." We nodded approvingly. We loved to climb trees.

"Or you could go back away from the trees and find a really big hill to accomplish the same thing."

"What else?" we queried.

"You could ask the trees."

"Ask the trees?"

"Yes, ask the trees if they are part of a really big family."

Sullenly, "Trees don't talk."

"Don't they?" Mother smiled. "You just might be pleasantly surprised."

"Well, they don't! Trees don't talk. Everybody knows that."

"Who's everybody?" We sank a little lower in our chairs. Hands on hips, Mother smiled and said, "Well, everybody doesn't know everything. Remember that."

We waited for more. "Run along now," she said.

With a sigh of relief, we quietly pushed our chairs back under the edge of the table and walked quickly toward the screened kitchen door, which was our escape to the outside world, a place free from lectures.

Behind us, we heard a chuckle, followed by "Say hello to the trees for me."

Though that exchange took place more than fifty years ago, the memory of that conversation is as fresh to me today, as though it had just occurred. And the lesson is no less powerful.

What do we really know about our 'own' trees, our 'own' personal forest? Are we standing too close to see the trees? And what does each of the trees denote to us? How do they impact us as a group, or forest?

Personally, I have always loved trees. As mentioned earlier, it was under the shaded, protective arms of a tree that my grandmother first began to teach me the native ways. So this was my tree of knowledge.

I also think of this particular tree as my tree of life, since it was where I was immersed into the native ways once more. I remember feeling as one with the tree. Trees have powerful healing energy and great wisdom. I remember being the recipient of all of the diverse energies, all the while learning the trick of invisibility within the camouflaging bulk of the tree.

The tree spoke with me and I listened. My grandmother spoke and I listened. Some trees have a reputation for shyness, but many trees I have known are not only great conversationalists, but great orators, as well.

Ask any Native American you know, and if they feel comfortable talking with you, they will confirm that trees are great communicators.

I have always been thankful to 'my' tree and others, for they do a great deal of good in the world. They are selfless. They give of themselves that we may enjoy shelter and be warm. They bring charm to any landscape. They house birds and squirrels—as well as countless others.

Trees give of themselves for medicines.

Most of all, they give life where life would not be possible by purifying the air.

I like to think that I can tell the forest from the trees, but, the truth is, I sometimes get so involved with a particular tree that I find myself lost, deep within the forest.

How do I find my way out of the forest? I listen to the trees singing. The younger trees, closest to the edge of the forest, may often be heard singing, while their elders, more introspective by nature, love to think great thoughts in the quiet of the deep woods.

Sometimes, as I gaze upon the trees, I fancy I hear the laughter in my mother's voice, wafting on a gentle breeze.

"Step away from the trees!"

Open the Floodgates To Your Future

"Open the floodgates to your future!"

"But what are the floodgates to my future? And where are they?"

"The floodgates to our future are many and varied, not to be taken lightly. You might think of them as ideas or concepts. You might think of them as the 'keys that unlock the hidden door to your future.'"

Some gates lie within—within our conscious and unconscious minds. The floodgates to our future lie within the time-tested fabric of our intrinsic integrity, our honesty and objectivity.

Some gates lie without—these gates are the physical manifestations of what we need to learn and how we integrate this knowledge with our 'inner knowledge.'

The floodgates to our future open one after the other, when the time is right, when we have learned what we must learn on that particular leg of our journey. As we progress through our lives, each lesson is learned through observation, coupled with success or failure. As we continue, we draw ever closer to a gradual understanding and melding of our personal truth. We begin to understand our place within a larger framework of a connection to all things, all beings, and all universal aspects.

This, then, is our reality. It is our power, it is our oneness. It is who we are.

Is there a secret to the opening of the floodgates? Of course! Isn't there always? OPEN the floodgates! Open your mind. Open your heart. When you have allowed your spirituality to open completely and with trust, when you have opened your innermost self with confidence to the floodgates of your future, you will be completely suffused with knowledge, love, and serenity.

"What is the most important floodgate to the future?"

"Love, always love."

"Never underestimate the power of love. Love cures all. Love heals all. Love is the agent that forges emotion into kinder reason, and becomes greater by so doing. Intelligence and reason, coupled with love, become the hallmarks of passion—and compassion.

Ultimately, love might be defined as the indefinable. Love is the intangible wellspring from which arise our passions, permeating our thoughts and galvanizing us to action.

Without love, who would we be? Let's not find out. Instead, open wide the floodgates of your future to the healing balm and ultimate redemption of love.

We human beings have always been, and continue to be, successful mutants. Our very survival has depended upon mutating. We have a built-in system for evolutionary changes to our physical makeup, our mental restructuring, and the inborn dawning of recognition for our spiritual path. This is no accident. We carry this incredible information safely tucked away, awaiting release at the proper time, within our DNA.

Physical visualization helps us to understand this reality. Imagine yourself looking out over a desert, broken up from time to time by amazing mesas and rock formations, with plateaus extending into the distance as far as you can see, like waves upon the sea. Some of these plateaus are higher than others.

We live by a series of plateaus and heights, peaks and valleys. For long periods of our evolutionary journey, we find ourselves seemingly making no progress at all, often appearing to simply 'march in place' for great lengths of time or, worse yet, falling back from the place where we are now, 'losing ground.' But after a time, inexplicably, we find ourselves once again forging ahead to yet a higher plateau.

This is all about cycling. Everything in our universe cycles, and continues to cycle, though we may be unable to detect the cycle.

We've all heard the story about the 'fast-draw cowboy' who, when asked to demonstrate his speed at drawing his gun from his holster, readily agreed. A crowd of curious onlookers waited, and waited, for him to demonstrate his 'fast-draw,' his speed with a gun. Time passed, and still they waited—impatiently. Finally, sensing their restlessness, the cowboy looked over the crowd and drawled, "You want to see it again?"

This 'tongue in cheek' cowboy story illustrates how an incredibly miniscule cycle may appear not to be moving at all, or so slowly as to be nearly stopped. Nothing could be further from the truth. In reality, the energy within this miniscule form is moving at a tremendous rate of speed.

Likewise, a cycle 'lost' in the great expanse of space might, theoretically, escape detection.

These cycling mutations have occurred universally, including Mother Earth, Father Sky, Grandfather Sun, and Grandmother Moon, for as long as they have existed. When man and all his counterparts—animal, plant, and mineral—came to live on and with Mother Earth, we also lived within the loosely-knit confines of cycles. The cycles, as well, were in a state of continuing mutation, changing as often as necessary to remain viable.

Today, we often find ourselves struggling to understand where we fit into the vast scheme of things. Most of us freely embrace the concept that, even now, we are an emerging species, constantly adapting in order to continue.

We may feel we are 'over-simplifying' by recognizing the basic pattern of our lives. We live on a plateau until it is no longer suitable, at which time we escalate to a higher plateau, remain there until it is no longer suitable, and continue, and continue, and continue, striving to reach ever higher to the next peak of evolution and learning. However great or small our understanding, this method of advancement is happening—all the time—and ultimately IN all time.

This One: "Is there an easy way to remember this?"

The Old Ones (with indulgent smiles): "What is—is."

This One: "What else?"

The Old Ones: "What will be—will be."

The Old Ones: "Let freedom sing."

This One: "Sing? Let freedom sing?"

The Old Ones (grinning): "Yes. Let freedom sing. And dance.

"Give up the ego."

"Realize what is truly important. Recognize what is truly necessary."

"Lighten your load. Do not carry excess baggage."

"More importantly, do not carry excess baggage for anyone else."

"Do not interfere with another's life path. You do not have the right to do so."

"Do not spend your life waiting. Tomorrow may not come."

"Life is a nebulous thing, a wisp of smoke blown on the wind. Enjoy it now."

"Do not wait for things to be perfect. Live and let live. Live now!"

"Choose to be happy. Listen to your heart. Live your personal truth."

"Don't be afraid to walk the road less traveled."

"Don't worry. Be happy."

"Be true to yourself and, therefore, to others."

"Be aware."

"Be thankful for the gifts Creator has given you."

"Give thanks to Creator, Wakan Tanka Tunka Silla.

This One: "Words to live by."

The Old Ones: "Always live into the higher self. Your life depends upon it. Your future depends upon it. And, ultimately, the salvation of Mother Earth and all her creatures depends upon it. Do not fail yourself. Do not fail Mother Earth and all her creatures."

The Old Ones: "Remember the dream that is life. Live into life. Celebrate life."

"Go forth, walking in a good way, and be happy."

This One: "We go from here!"

The Old Ones: "Do not forget—remember always...

Live into the higher self! Aho!"

Lightning Source UK Ltd.
Milton Keynes UK
UKOW04f1912200116

266822UK00001B/116/P